POLITICAL PORTRAITS

GENERAL EDITOR
KENNETH O. MORGAN

LORD PALMERSTON

MURIEL E. CHAMBERLAIN

GPC
BOOKS

GPC Books is an imprint of the University of Wales Press, 6 Gwennyth Street, Cardiff
CF2 4YD

First published in 1987

British Library Cataloguing in Publication Data
Chamberlain, M.E.
Lord Palmerston—(Political Portraits, v.I).
1. Palmerston, Henry John Temple. Viscount.
I. Title II. Series
941 081'092'4
ISBN 0-7083-0978-X
ISBN 0-7083-0973-9 Pbk

Cover Design: T.C. Evans Design Graphics
The publishers wish to acknowledge the advice and assistance given by the Design
Department of the Welsh Books Council which is supported by the Welsh Arts Council.

Set by Quality Phototypesetting, Bristol
Printed in Great Britain at the Bath Press, Avon

Contents

Editor's Foreword

The aim of this open-ended series of short biographies is to offer personal portraits of the decisive figures in the making of British politics over the past two hundred years. It will range over leading practitioners of politics, from Britain and Ireland (and probably the commonwealth/empire as well) who have vitally shaped our public affairs in the nineteenth and twentieth centuries. Its premise, of course, is that people and biographies are vitally important as explanatory keys to the past. Too often, historians tend to see the course of historical change in terms of vague impersonal factors, evolutionary patterns, underlying themes, even that Scylla and Charybdis of historical understanding, 'forces' and 'trends'. The impact of the disciplines of economics, sociology or anthropology is often taken as reinforcing this tendency, and helping to obliterate flesh-and-blood human beings from our map of the past.

Now, no-one would seriously dispute the enrichment of historical studies that has resulted from the stimulus of other disciplines. At the same time, it can hardly be questioned that the role of key individuals, locally and regionally as well as nationally, has been crucial in shaping the rhythms and speed of our political development in the years since the twin impact of industrialization and representative democracy. The growth of our political parties are impossible to visualize without the personal imprint of Gladstone, Disraeli or Keir Hardie. The course of wars, and their consequences, would have been totally different if Lloyd George or Churchill had never lived. Without Parnell or de Valera, modern Ireland would not have emerged in its present form. Even in the 1980s, the dominance of Mrs Thatcher confirms anew the powerful impulses that can be released by the authority or whim of one determined individual.

So there need be no apology for offering a new series of biographies, brief but authoritative, all written by expert scholars, designed for the intelligent general reader as well as for the student or the specialist, as launch-pads for political and historical understanding. Portraits of individuals, naturally, open up wider social, cultural or intellectual themes. They also help to make history fun—vibrant, vivid, accessible. They may also be a means to a deeper understanding of our world. It should always be remembered that Karl Marx himself, whose influence is so frequently taken as eliminating individuals entirely from history in favour of the rise and conflict of social classes, actually took the reverse view himself. 'History', Marx wrote, 'is nothing but the activity of men in pursuit of their ends.' Some of these men—and women—and the ends they pursued, achieved, missed out on, or simply forgot, are illustrated in this series.

The astonishing and paradoxical career of Lord Palmerston is examined here by Dr Muriel Chamberlain of Swansea, herself a major authority on modern international and imperial history. 'Pam' is frequently presented as a kind of permanent incubus in Victorian Britain, an eighteenth-century breakwater against change who had miraculously survived into the later nineteenth century. Yet Palmerston was also a vigorous and progressive administrator, adroit in using and creating public opinion, with remarkably close links with the popular press. His lengthy career stretched from the interest politics of Pittite days to the dawn of the modern Liberal Party. It extended from the Georgian country gentleman to the modern organization man and *apparatchik*. In spite of himself, Pam became the catalyst of a more contemporary age. Overseas, he is usually linked with crude stereotypes of gunboat diplomacy and national greatness, contemptuously imposing his will on foreigners from the Don Pacifico affair in Greece to the Opium Wars in China. When Herbert Morrison became Foreign Secretary in March 1951, he took down from the shelves a biography of Palmerston by Harry Bell to bolster his resolve; shortly he offered the world his own twentieth-century version of updated Palmerstonianism in the Abadan oil crisis.

Yet Palmerston had a broad sense of ideas and context. His view of Britain's 'national interest' was closely linked with more mundane considerations—Britain's need for overseas trade and investment especially in the Near and Far East, the value of balanced peace and stability in continental Europe, and the maintenance of constitutionalism. The irony was that, especially after the revolutions of 1848, Palmerston found his foreign policy increasingly determined by others. The rise of a united Germany and Italy, pan-Slavism in the Balkans, the rising industrial might of America were already, in his own lifetime, disturbing the facade of British imperial greatness. Palmerston's world was dissolving in the era of Bismarck and Lincoln, assuming that it had ever existed in the first place. The 'Pam' that Dr Chamberlain presents, therefore, is a much more interesting and complex figure than the crude John Bull stereotype of legend. The superficial bluster concealed a diplomatic finesse and inner caution, a man who had to give way discreetly before domestic opinion and external pressures, a foreign secretary and prime minister whose reputation for bravado and provocation was often at odds with the reality. Even Palmerston usually preferred 'jaw jaw' to 'war war', to adopt Churchill's phrase. So Palmerston, like the nation he symbolized, with its supposed 'Victorian values', was more multi-dimensional than popular impressions suggested. It is perhaps not too fanciful to see in him the first political leader who had to grapple, even in the mid-Victorian heyday, with the early premonitions of British national decline.

The man and his legacy, then contain contradictions and puzzles. What undoubtedly survives, though, is an exuberant, colourful, inexhaustible personality, full of fun, capable of bounding up the stars to the ladies' gallery of the Commons at the age of eighty. In the hothouse world of high politics, for 'Pam' cheerfulness always kept breaking in. This, too, is an essential part of the portrait drawn by Dr Chamberlain in her fascinating and authoritative book.

KENNETH O. MORGAN
The Queen's College, Oxford

Acknowledgements

My thanks are due, first, to Her Majesty the Queen for her gracious permission to consult and quote from material in the Royal Archives; secondly, to Lord Brabourne for giving me permission on behalf of the Trustees of the Broadland Archives to consult and quote from the Broadlands Papers, now at Southampton University Library, but the in the care of the Historical Manuscripts Commission. Acknowledgement is also due to the Trustees of the British Library for the quotations from the Aberdeen and Bright Papers; the Earl of Clarendon, Sir Charles Graham and the Bodleian Library for the use of the Clarendon and Graham Papers. The Public Record Office papers are crown copyright.

1

Palmerston: The Man and the Legend

Everyone thinks that he or she knows Lord Palmerston. He was the rumbustious embodiment of Victorian foreign policy, so much easier to understand than his political associates or rivals, Sir Robert Peel or the fourth Earl of Aberdeen, serious remote men, who could not project themselves even to their contemporary public. In fact the third Viscount Palmerston was an extraordinarily complex character. Contradictions meet the biographer at every turn. How did the diffident young man, unsure of his own abilities, and apparently content with minor office for twenty years (and this in a period when young men often went quickly to the top), turn into the John Bullish old man of legend?

At times his policy seemed almost schizophrenic. In December 1853 *The Times* and the *Morning Herald* argued in their editorials whether it was correct to say, 'In his policy abroad he is a Liberal, at home a Tory.'[1] It is a problem which since has exercised the minds of generations of historians (and examination candidates). How could a man who championed constitutional governments abroad and became the *bête noire* of European conservatives, to the point where they nicknamed him 'the Devil's son', be the almost life-long opponent of parliamentary reform at home? His support for the 1832 Reform Act was luke-warm. As he grew older his attitude became more rigid. By the 1850s he seemed to have an almost pathological fear of the masses. 'Can it be expected', he asked in one outburst 'that men who murder their children for 9£ to be spent on drink will not sell their vote for whatever they can get for it?'[2] In the end even committed reformers, like John Bright, gave up and waited for the old man to die.

Yet at the same time he was capable of generous impulses of sympathy for the unfortunate or oppressed. He was an early convert to the cause of

Catholic Emancipation, even though it was a politically dangerous question and one which seemed likely to cost him the Cambridge University seat, on which he had set his heart. He was converted a little more slowly to opposition to the slave trade but, once convinced, he crusaded all his life for its final extinction, even when this created diplomatic difficulties and was at odds with other international objectives. He allowed himself to be convinced by a practical demonstration[3] of the evils of child labour and supported factory reform. At the very end of his life, he was arguing that the Foreign Office clerks should be allowed Saturday afternoon off because men were not 'mere Machines which would regularly do a given Quantity of Work in a given Time like a Steam Engine' but 'moral and intellectual agents, and . . . the work performed by them in a given Time, depends much on the cheerfulness & good will with which it is done'.[4]

As Home Secretary in 1852–5 he was an energetic reformer, not only introducing the first Smoke Abatement Act in London, but concerning himself with a wide variety of penal and health reforms. But when he became Prime Minister in 1855 he seemed to have lost all interest in domestic reform. He notoriously remarked to Goschen in 1864 that they could not 'go on adding to the statute book *ad infinitum*'[5] and in fact his two premierships were almost devoid of reforming legislation, apart from William Gladstone's financial measures, of many of which the Prime Minister himself did not approve.

The simplest explanation – that Palmerston, like many men, just suffered from hardening of the arteries as he grew older and became more and more conservative and unwilling to see changes in the system with which he was familiar – will not fit. In foreign affairs he became more and more radical, or at least was quite willing to allow himself to appear so. In the first two foreign questions which really seem to have impinged upon his consciousness in the 1820s, the Greek war of independence and the civil war in Portugal, he reacted rather as he did over the slave trade or child labour. Once having looked at the facts, he quickly made up his mind where the truth lay and felt a generous impulse to support what he had no doubt was the right side. But during his long years in charge of British foreign policy, as Foreign Secretary, 1830–4, 1835–41, 1846–51 and as Prime Minister, 1855–8, 1859–65, he usually acted (as distinct from spoke) with innate caution. Even at the end of his life he clearly regarded the Vienna Settlement of 1815 as the basis of the European order.[6] But, against this, must be set the fact that from the great revolutionary crisis of 1848–9 onwards he was quite happy to accept (even to play up to) a public image of a radical statesman who would throw his weight on the side of what a slightly later generation would call 'peoples rightly struggling to be free'. It was this supposed radicalism which put him at odds not only with European conservatives but also with the Court in Britain.

Palmerston (or again perhaps one must say, the later Palmerston) was a pugnacious man. He was also a very intelligent man. He was extremely good at bluff, although he occasionally overplayed his hand, as with Russell in 1851 or with Bismarck in 1864. But his most conspicuous quality seems to have been that of sheer energy, which he inherited from both his parents. He both worked and played extraordinarily hard. This may explain one paradox in contemporary views of him.

He was a most industrious man, who set out to master every detail of his official brief, whether at the War Office as a young man or at the Foreign Office later. His private secretary, Charles Barrington, had a story that the drivers of the horse-drawn omnibuses would point out Palmerston at his desk in his house in Piccadilly as they went past and that one of them remarked ''E earns 'is wages; I never come by without seeing 'im 'ard at it.'[7] More importantly, his mastery of detail made it very difficult for either foreign diplomats or his Cabinet colleagues to argue against him, particularly as his knowledge and experience grew from long years in office. At the same time contemporaries accused him of neglecting his official duties for his social life and on several occasions, some of them important, this does seem to have been the case.[8] It was notorious that Palmerston would often keep foreign diplomats waiting and some writers have assumed that this was a deliberate tactic to gain a psychological advantage; but more recent revelations suggest that it also arose from his determined pursuit of private pleasures. The final paradox of this very complex man is that, although he was Prime Minister for nearly ten years in the middle of Queen Victoria's reign, in his private life he flouted almost every Victorian convention.

Palmerston has attracted many biographers, but the popular twentieth-century picture derives very largely from Philip Guedalla's famous life published in 1926 – even though a later writer, Donald Southgate, quite rightly calls it 'a work of art rather than a biography'. Guedalla saw him as a larger-than-life, eighteenth-century figure, who somehow survived into the nineteenth, and who consistently dominated those around him whether in Britain or in Europe.

In 1951 Sir Charles Webster produced his massive two-volume study of Palmerston's conduct of foreign policy between 1830 and 1841. Although it was not published until after the Second World War Webster had, as he says in his preface, completed the analysis of the material and come to his conclusions by 1939.[9] On the face of it, Webster's work could not be more different from Guedalla's. Where Guedalla is impressionistic, Webster is exhaustive; where Guedalla is interested in painting an artist's picture of a whole cultural milieu, Webster is interested in all the technical minutiae of diplomacy. But the same basic assumptions underlie both books. Both men admired Palmerston and both saw him as the dominant man of his time.

Searching modern criticism of Palmerston's policies began with Gavin Henderson. Henderson's work too was interrupted by the Second World War and his death in an air crash towards the end of the war meant that he never published a comprehensive study of Palmerston or his period but his important, although scattered, papers on the subject were printed under the title *Crimean War Diplomacy and Other Essays* in 1947. Henderson asked penetrating questions about the consistency of Palmerston's policy and in particular about the relationship between Palmerston and public opinion. He quoted with approval the view of a nineteenth-century writer, Justin McCarthy, 'Palmerston never really guided, but always followed, the English public, even in foreign affairs' and concluded, 'Palmerston stimulated passions that he failed to control, and favoured a policy the consequences of which he did not foresee.'[10]

This approach attracted a riposte from Donald Southgate in his '*The Most English Minister. . .': the policies and politics of Palmerston,* published in 1966. Southgate's book was not strictly a biography. It began for practical purposes in 1828 and was essentially a study of Palmerston when he held high office. Southgate was not uncritical of Palmerston on some points but he too was essentially an admirer and, in particular, he attacked the idea that Palmerston could ever be regarded simply as the reflection of the English nation at a particular moment in its history, of a Britain which was 'less critical of itself than it had been, or was to be for decades and was proportionately more critical, more arrogantly critical . . . of others'. 'That Palmerston was sometimes a bully and often a showman', he wrote 'is conceded. That he was a poseur is not.'[11]

Among the myriad biographies of Palmerston, four must be singled out for mention. The first is the official biography, begun by Henry Lytton Bulwer, later Lord Dalling, and finished by Evelyn Ashley. Bulwer was both an MP and a career diplomat (not an uncommon combination in Victorian times), who had frequently served under Palmerston. He had had his differences with his chief but he liked and admired him. Particularly when discussing foreign policy, Bulwer was essentially presenting the case for the defence. His underlying assumption was simple: Palmerston had been doing his best for Britain, aided by men like Bulwer himself, and it was still possible to demonstrate that they had been right, at least most of the time.

Ashley, who completed the work after Bulwer's death, was at first sight an improbable biographer for Palmerston. He was, after all, the son of the great Victorian evangelical, Lord Shaftesbury, hardly the most likely man to be writing a hagiographic life of 'Lord Cupid'. The connection was a family one. Ashley was the step-grandson (if rumour was correct, the grandson) of Palmerston. His father had married Emily (Minnie) Cowper, the daughter of Lady Cowper, for so long Palmerston's mistress and subsequently wife. Ashley's part of the biography consisted almost entirely of extracts from Palmerston's own letters and writings, linked by a few narrative passages. Both Bulwer and Ashley had the advantage of free access to Palmerston's private papers but they did not have the opportunity a modern scholar would have of consulting the official archives of the period – although this was offset to some extent by Bulwer's first-hand knowledge of many of the relevant diplomatic transactions. The great virtue of the Bulwer–Ashley biography (apart from Bulwer's status as an eye witness) was that in its five volumes it made available an extensive selection of Palmerston's private papers which, until recently, have not been easily accessible to scholars. As such it has remained an indispensable quarry for historians.

The next really important biography was the two-volume work of an American scholar, H.C. Bell, published in 1936. This was not based on Palmerston's private papers but on the official records which were now open for inspection and, to a much lesser extent, on some other collections of private papers, which had not been available to Bulwer and Ashley. Bell was typical of the inter-war school of diplomatic historians, when much classic work was produced in that field. Although it was a biography, not simply a foreign policy study, it invites comparison with Webster's work. It was serious, detailed and comprehensive and remains the most solid study covering the whole of Palmerston's life. Bell offers his own judgement of Palmerston in his last few pages. He diagnoses the mainspring of Palmerston's policy as being quite simply nationalism and sees this as self-justifying. 'Palmerston', he wrote, 'can best be understood as an exponent of early and mid-nineteenth-century nationalism.' This explained why he was always prepared for reconciliation with Russell, who several times treated him very badly but basically shared his opinions on foreign policy, but could never really come to terms with Gladstone, who had a different

world view. Bell thought it was self-justifying because Palmerston was
seeking a moral, not a material, pre-eminence for England. He mildly
rebuked Palmerston's fellow-countrymen for not appreciating him
sufficiently. 'Englishmen of his own day', he wrote 'stood too close to him
for detached analysis.' It was left to the editor of the Vienna *Debatte* to
understand him fully when he said, 'In the clash of principles and
convictions he recognised only one – the interest of England – and he
served this with sacrificing devotion. Whatever could advance England's
power and greatness was law, in following up which he left all other
considerations out of sight.'[12]

That nationalism (moral or not) was self-validating seemed obvious to
many people in the 1930s. By the 1970s, perspectives had somewhat
changed. Jasper Ridley's *Lord Palmerston* brought a breath of fresh air
into Palmerstonian studies. Like Guedalla's biography, it was a lively
book which could be read with pleasure by those who had no specialist
interest in nineteenth-century history. It had an element of iconoclasm in
it. Palmerston emerged from it as an attractive figure but an entirely
fallible and human one. Ridley did not start from the assumption that
either Palmerston or his country was always right. The treatment of certain
episodes came as a distinct surprise to those who still retained a traditional
view of Britain as a powerful, liberal constitutional force intervening for
the good in the murky affairs of nineteenth-century Europe. The
opportunistic element of his policy in 1847–9 was very apparent. He was
lucky to escape a diplomatic humiliation in Switzerland in 1847, similar to
that which he suffered over Schleswig-Holstein in 1864. Continental
statesmen had good reasons for complaining that Britain had double
standards, loudly condemning Austria for her actions in Hungary or Italy
while employing similar methods against her own dissidents in Ireland or
the Ionian Islands.

The most recent major work on Palmerston is Kenneth Bourne's
biography which so far only goes up to 1841. It is based on a detailed
examination of both the official archives and of private papers, including
Palmerston's own, and largely supersedes earlier works. Professor Bourne
has aimed to avoid repeating some of the minute examination of foreign
affairs undertaken by Webster from the official archives in the 1930s and
has concentrated, at least in this first volume, upon Palmerston the man.
He is the first scholar to be able to use some of Palmerston's private diaries
and he has also tried to set Palmerston very much in the context of his
times. The word which rises most readily to mind to describe the social
setting in which Palmerston operated is the contemporary slang 'rackety'.

Palmerston was often in financial difficulties. He was also a (not always successful) Casanova, whose almost obsessive search for sexual satisfaction, recorded in a transparent code in his diaries, suggests some basic insecurity.

Palmerston was never entirely trusted by those who knew him well. Bourne's new evidence goes some way to explain why they always felt that he was a little unstable. The distrust extended into his public as well as his private life. There were those who sneered that Palmerston did not like being out of office and, by implication, would make any sort of deal which would keep him in place. Even *The Times'* obituary admitted 'It has been said that he was constant only in the retention of office . . . that his one principle was that of the Vicar of Bray.'[13] His long career, when he was in office for approximately fifty-eight of his sixty-four adult years, by turns Tory, Canningite, Whig and even 'Liberal', certainly gave his enemies plenty of ammunition.

The same charge of opportunism has been levelled against his conduct of foreign affairs. The Prussian envoy, Baron von Bunsen, once said of him, 'He has no principle and he has no heart.' The Duke of Argyll, a shrewd man who sat in a number of Cabinets with Palmerston, was sufficiently struck by the remark to comment, 'Palmerston was not, in the ordinary meaning of the word, an unprincipled politician. He was honest in his purposes, and truthful in his prosecution of them . . . But what Bunsen meant was true − he had no ideals for the future of the world, and had a profound distrust of those who professed to be guided by such ideals.'[14] There is more to the charge than regret at the obvious fact that a Foreign Secretary must constantly adjust his policy to circumstances over which he has, at best, limited control. In that sense no one could reasonably complain that Palmerston was an opportunist. Up to a point, he had to be. The charge is rather that Palmerston's understanding of the issues was always superficial. Interestingly Bourne, although admiring his tactical skill, reaches much the same conclusion as many contemporary critics did. 'He lacked', he says 'qualities of moral leadership' and 'he went with the tide of public opinion.'[15]

2

The Temple Family

The Temples were said to be descended from Leofric, the eleventh-century Earl of Mercia, and his wife Lady Godiva, and the eagles on their coat of arms were supposed to commemorate the fact. The story had been laughed out of court even in Victorian times[1] but some thought it a peculiarly appropriate descent for that quintessential Englishman, the third Viscount Palmerston. It can be asserted with more confidence that they were a Warwickshire gentry family, who first rose to prominence under the Tudors. One, William Temple, was secretary to Sir Philip Sidney. 'Sir Philip', it is said 'died in his arms at Arnheim, and dying commended him to the Earl of Essex, beside leaving him an annuity of thirty pounds.'[2] Temple accompanied Essex to Ireland on his expedition in 1599, thus forming the first connection with the island which was to provide the Palmerstons with their title and most of their income. Temple was inevitably involved in Essex's disgrace but his friends secured the Mastership of Trinity College, Dublin, for him in 1609.

His son, Sir John Temple, became Master of the Rolls in Ireland and was a leading parliamentarian during the Civil War. He was granted substantial estates confiscated from Irish Catholic royalists after Cromwell's campaign there. His eldest son, Sir William Temple, became a famous statesman and diplomatist under William III but it was his second son, John, who maintained the Irish connection. In 1689 he was attainted as a traitor and his lands declared forfeit by the Irish Parliament, which still supported James II, but after the battle of the Boyne the Protestant Ascendancy was once again secure. John became Attorney-General of Ireland and Speaker of the Irish House of Commons, as well as acquiring further confiscated lands. In 1723 his son, Henry, was created Viscount Palmerston of Palmerston in the County of Dublin.

As an Irish peer, the first Lord Palmerston was not entitled to sit in the House of Lords at Westminster but he remained eligible to sit in the House of Commons there. For most of his adult life he represented a succession of rotten boroughs, East Grinstead, Bossiney and Weobley. He married Anne, the daughter of Abraham Houblon, a Governor of the Bank of England. From his father he inherited a house at East Sheen in Surrey and he himself bought a pleasant country house, Broadlands, near Romsey in Hampshire, which his grandson was to enlarge and embellish with the help of Henry Holland and Capability Brown.

The first Viscount Palmerston died in 1757. His son had continued the family connection with the City of London by marrying Jane, the daughter of John Barnard, who had been Lord Mayor in 1737–8. The son predeceased his father and the title was inherited by his eighteen-year-old grandson, another Henry. The second Viscount Palmerston had some modest political ambitions. He sat in Parliament for forty years for various pocket boroughs and held minor offices at the Admiralty and the Treasury. His politics were Whig of a conventional kind, supporting the government and the traditions of the 'Glorious Revolution' of 1688. Towards the end of his life, when the French Revolution and the revolutionary wars had broken out, he drifted into supporting the Younger Pitt.

By then, it was clear that he saw himself as a cultured man-about-town rather than as an active politician. He was mildly, and intelligently interested in the theatre, art, sculpture and the new scientific discoveries. He installed a telescope at Broadlands and corresponded with the distinguished astronomer, John Herschell. His friends included David Garrick, Sir Joshua Reynolds, Edward Gibbon, Richard Brinsley Sheridan, Sir Joseph Banks, the scientist and formidable President of the Royal Society, and the great Dr Samuel Johnson. He was an active member of the Society of Dilettanti which, by the late eighteenth century, was the most important patron of classical archaeology in Britain. It is not perhaps surprising that his son, the third Viscount, sometimes hankered for his father's relaxed and pleasant lifestyle and this almost certainly played its part, although probably not a decisive part, in his apparent contentment with junior office.

In 1767 the second Viscount married Frances Poole, a connection of the powerful Pelham family, but she died two years later in childbirth and the child did not survive. His second marriage, in 1783, became the subject of romantic legend which was perpetuated even by Bulwer. According to this, Lord Palmerston was thrown from his horse when riding in Dublin and carried in to a nearby house, where he was nursed so devotedly by the daughter of the house, a Miss Mary Mee, that he fell in love with her and married her. Some reports said Mr Mee was a hatter and Bulwer had to apologize for calling him 'a tradesman' in his first edition.[3] Alas for legend, the Mees were merchants in the City of London and lived in Gloucestershire, not Dublin. Palmerston had known Mary since she was a child since the families were not merely acquainted but distantly related. Oddly enough, the riding accident story seems to be almost an inversion of the truth. Palmerston had been driving a phaeton which overturned with Mary and her sister in it. Mary's elbow was dislocated and, although she quickly recovered, Palmerston was sufficiently contrite to become very attentive. They were married in Bath in January 1783.

The marriage again consolidated the family connection with the City of London, but with some unfortunate consequences this time. Mary's brother, Benjamin, although a governor of the Bank of England, had incredibly bad financial judgement and on several occasions his new brother-in-law had to rescue him from the consequences of his follies. Palmerston himself was comfortably off, rather than rich by the standards of the time. His income came mainly from his Irish estates, principally in County Sligo, which provided him with rents of about £6,000. He drew a further £2,000 from the rents of lands in Hampshire, Yorkshire and Northamptonshire and about £3,000 from a variety of investments. His interest in his Irish estates was almost entirely confined to receiving rents and he paid only four short visits there during the whole of his life.

His marriage to Mary Mee, contracted when he was forty-three and she twenty-eight, proved to be a happy one. There were five children. Henry John – Harry to his family, who was to succeed as third Viscount – was born in London on 20 October 1784. His birth was followed by that of Frances (1786), William (1788), Mary (1789) and Elizabeth (1790). The children, and especially the two brothers, remained close all their lives. The second Viscount's enthusiasm for scientific advance cost Mary her life. Jenner had not yet invented a safe form of vaccination against small pox, using cow pox. Instead those who dared were innoculated with an attenuated form of live small pox. It was a risk worth taking when mortality and disfigurement from small pox were a scourge, but it could go wrong. Mary died. Harry, who had been innoculated earlier, seems to have been quite seriously ill. Various accounts suggest that Harry was far from a robust child and his mother's constant concern for his health may not have been mere maternal fussiness.

Interesting sidelights on the young Temples at this time come from Gilbert Elliot, the first Earl of Minto, who was so fond of Harry that he came to regard him almost as his own son. He wrote to his wife in 1789, 'Even Harry, who used to look so washy, has got quite stout, with a fine high colour. He is now a vastly pretty boy, still in petticoats, but they are measuring him for his first breeches to-day.' The children were naturally kept mainly in the nursery at Broadlands. Their relations with their parents were unusually warm and close but they were not yet ready to participate in their parents' rather feverish social life, centring on the great house at East Sheen, described by Minto as 'a prodigious great magnificent old-fashioned house, with pleasure-grounds consisting of seventy acres – pieces of water, artificial mounds, and so forth.'[4]

Fashionable opinion was unanimous that Lady Palmerston was 'agreeable', although there are also hints that some found her a little vulgar. Sheridan's wife paid her the doubtful compliment of saying that she did not put on airs 'tho' she did squeeze thru' the City Gates into a Viscountess'. She was certainly not discreet. Lord Glenbervie said she was 'a great protectress of the class of demi-reps', who invited women of 'equivocal character' to her parties. 'Junkety' was the word which occurred to several contemporaries to describe life at East Sheen and one added that 'that cannot be avoided . . . in any place inhabited by the Palmerstons or any of their family.' Even the sympathetic Lord Minto was driven to comment, 'I never saw any two people make such a toil of pleasure, as both he and she. She seems completely worn down by her raking, but is always eager for the next labour.' Like his more famous son, the second Viscount was a 'fidgetty' man who could not bear to be still.[5]

Some of his restlessness took the form of a constant desire to travel. This provided the first great adventure of the young Harry's life. When possible the Viscount took his wife and children with him and even the outbreak of the French Revolution did not deter him from visiting the continent. He had been travelling with his wife and eldest son in Germany and the Low Countries in 1789 and they witnessed the first revolutionary outbreaks in Liège and Brussels but in July 1792 the whole family, with a large retinue of servants, left London to travel to Italy by way of France. They arrived in Paris on 1 August. The Tuileries had already been attacked on 20 June but, in a rather ghastly parody of normality, Palmerston and his wife were presented to Louis XVI and Marie Antoinette by the British ambassador. Lady Palmerston noted compassionately that the Dauphin, who was about to disappear for ever into a revolutionary prison, was a boy about Harry's age.

Even the Palmerstons were rather alarmed by the situation and left Paris on 7 August, having obtained travel documents from the revolutionary authorities at the Hôtel de Ville. The first carriage, containing Lord and Lady Palmerston and Harry, drove out of the city without serious difficulty; but the other carriages with the servants and younger children were stopped in the working class and radical Faubourg St Antoine and only released after the intervention of a local revolutionary leader. The Palmerstons were on their way to Lyons before the Tuileries was again attacked and Louis XVI finally deposed on 10 August, but their problems were not over. They found Lyons too convulsed with revolutionary excitement, particularly as war had just broken out with Austria and Prussia. Lady Palmerston wrote that, as they set out from Lyons, they were 'much incommoded in the first stages by crowds of people going to join the armies, who, being the very refuse of the mob and under no discipline, were unpleasant fellow travellers'.[6] The third Viscount was a small boy at the time and there is no record of how he felt about the matter, but it is not perhaps fanciful to suppose that some of his later fear of revolution and of the 'lower classes' sprang from his experiences in France in 1792.

The Palmerstons reached neutral Switzerland safely and went on to Italy, arriving in Naples just before Christmas. They passed an agreeable winter there and struck up a friendship with the British ambassador, Sir William Hamilton, who was, like the second Viscount Palmerston, an assiduous collector of classical antiquities, and with his wife, Lady Hamilton, not yet notorious as Nelson's mistress but already enjoying a rather dubious reputation. Since Naples was considered unhealthy in hot weather, they spent the summer of 1793 in Switzerland. Returning to Naples in the autumn, young Harry was struck down by a serious fever in Verona but recovered sufficiently for the family to be back in Naples by Christmas. In May 1794 they began the journey back to England but, since England too was now at war with France, they had to travel by a circuitous route through Austria and Germany. On the way they stayed for a month near The Hague and visited the Duke of York's army which was preparing to defend Holland, unsuccessfully, against the French.

It is impossible to know what effect these early travels had on the young Harry. His parents' journals and letters suggest that so much of it was spent among British communities abroad that, quite apart from his youth, he may have had little chance to form any real impression of continental life. It did not prevent him from growing up into one of Britain's most insular statesman and he showed no great enthusiasm for foreign travel as an adult. It did, however, leave him with an enviable command of some European languages. The second Viscount seems to have hoped that both his sons might enter the diplomatic service and he therefore set about providing them with a good linguistic training. In 1788 he engaged the services of a French governess, Thérèse Mercier, who was probably the niece of a well-regarded French writer, Louis Sebastien Mercier, and who remained with the family for many years. While in Naples he engaged an Italian tutor, Gaetano Ravizotti (known as Señor Gaetano within the family), who was said to be a political refugee from Rome. It is tempting to suppose that Palmerston first acquired his sympathy for Italian national aspirations from Señor Gaetano but, unfortunately, there is no hard evidence about Gaetano's political views. He was a distinguished scholar who taught Palmerston some Spanish as well as Italian. As an undergraduate at Edinburgh, Harry tried to learn German but found it much harder than the Romance languages he had learnt as a child and never mastered it.

When the family returned to Britain in October 1794, it was judged to be time for Harry to go to Harrow. Despite his comparative fluency in modern languages, Harry was behind his contemporaries in the classics, and in the winter of 1794–5 Señor Gaetano seems to have given him what amounted to a crash course in Greek and Latin. Even so, when Harry arrived at Harrow in the spring of 1795 he had to be taught privately for some months by his housemaster, Dr Thomas Bromley. Harry seems to have been unusually lucky for the period in his teachers and he quickly settled down under the almost parental care of Dr and Mrs Bromley.

Harrow had only recently become a really fashionable school and its success was largely due to Joseph Drury who had been its headmaster since 1785. It was still small with only 139 pupils in 1796 but Harry Temple's contemporaries included two other future prime ministers, Frederick Robinson, later Earl of Ripon, and George Gordon (then Lord Haddo) later Earl of Aberdeen, as well as several other future cabinet ministers, Lords Spencer and Haddington among them. Robert Peel, who was a few years younger, went to Harrow the summer Harry left. Even in those days the relations between Temple and Haddo seem to have been those of rivalry, gleefully (and perhaps exaggeratedly) remembered by their contemporaries later in life. The best-known story is that of Temple worsting Haddo in a pillow fight but it is balanced by one of Haddo locking Temple in an inner room without a candle until he was heard intoning the words of the Collect, 'Lighten our darkness, Oh Lord we beseech thee.' Temple was more annoyed by the fact that Haddo was preferred to him to deliver a classical oration in the presence of admiring families and friends in July 1800. As Temple had been allowed to orate on two previous occasions, his pique seems rather exaggerated, but honour was saved when he was allowed instead to recite Thomas Grey's 'The Bard', the stirring tale of a Welsh bard who denounces Edward I's conquest of Wales and curses the House of Plantagenet. It was a popular piece at the time but there is a certain irony in it. As Jasper Ridley remarked, 'It was the last time in his life that Harry Temple denounced English imperialism.'[7]

Apart from a useful training in public speaking, perhaps partly inspired by Joseph Drury's devotion to the theatre, Temple received an adequate grounding in the classics and acquired some basic knowledge of mathematics. Judging by the idiosyncratic spelling of his schoolboy letters, good English had a low priority at Harrow. The school was still, despite Drury's efforts, a rough-and-ready place but Palmerston always retained an affection for his old school, of which he was in later years an active governor, and was inclined to be contemptuous of those who had not been licked into shape by the public school system. As a fourteen-year-old schoolboy he had explained rather priggishly to a friend that the fashionable vices of drinking and swearing held no attractions for him. In fact, in a hard-drinking age, Palmerston was always a comparatively abstemious man and perhaps he always had too ready a wit to need to descend to mere obscenities. For the rest he seems to have been a competent sportsman, enjoying his cricket, swimming, tennis and skating to which, as he grew up, was added that other fashionable pastime, shooting. He was not adverse to occasional fisticuffs which were expected of any spirited public schoolboy of the period, although Augustus Clifford's story of his great fight with a boy called Thomas Salisbury, reputedly 'twice his size', obviously lost nothing in the telling. Perhaps more genuinely indicative of his character at Harrow was the recollection, also attested by Clifford, who had been his fag, that Temple was a 'merciful and indulgent' fag-master. The general testimony seems to have been that he was a good-natured, well-liked boy.

The second Viscount apparently believed that only limited advantages could be derived from a public school and he took his son away before he reached his sixteenth birthday. The obvious next step would have been the Grand Tour but in 1800 Europe was closed to British travellers by the Napoleonic wars. Palmerston therefore decided that his son should do what other young men of good family were doing and go to Scotland instead. The Scottish universities accepted pupils at a younger age than the English universities and they were also academically better. Edinburgh in particular had benefitted from the Scottish Renaissance of the late eighteenth century which had produced great figures like the political economist, Adam Smith.

It was arranged that Harry should board in the house of Adam Smith's spiritual heir, Professor Dugald Stewart, at a cost of £400 a year.[8] Lord and Lady Palmerston accompanied Harry on a leisurely progress to Edinburgh in the autumn of 1800, which also included visits to Loch Lomond and other parts of Scotland. Lady Palmerston insisted on remaining in Edinburgh for a whole month to see her son safely settled in. Stewart had previously played host to Lord Henry Petty, later Marquess of Lansdowne, and John Ward, later Earl of Dudley. Lord John Russell arrived in Edinburgh soon after Palmerston but boarded with another professor, John Playfair. It meant a good deal more to Harry that the following year the Mintos took a house in Edinburgh and he was welcome to spend time with their son, Gilbert, later second Earl of Minto, and Gilbert's attractive sisters.

Edinburgh at this time had a somewhat radical reputation, but Lady Malmesbury, another close family friend, ridiculed the idea that Harry and Gilbert would be in any danger from that. She wrote to Gilbert's father. 'As to Jacobinism, it is all stuff everywhere. A boy of nineteen may be seduced by a fair face, or led into gaming, or drinking, or racing, but nobody at that age cares about politics that is worth a farthing.' Lady Malmesbury seemed to be correct. The Stewart household, in which Mrs Stewart firmly mothered her charges, was a happy one and Temple quickly settled in. He was determined to work hard and the general opinion of him at this time was that he was, if anything, too serious and sober a young man. Lady Minto said of him, 'He is charming, having no fault or failing, unless it be a want of the spirits belonging to his age.' Lord Minto was equally enthusiastic, telling Lady Palmerston, 'Diligence, capacity, total freedom from vice of any sort, gentle and kind disposition, cheerfulness, pleasantness, and perfect sweetness, are in the catalogue of properties by which we may advertise him if he should be lost.'[9] Even allowing for some disposition to flatter a young man to his parents, it sounds singularly unlike the later Palmerston.

In the meantime, he followed courses in mathematics, various sciences, history and philosophy, kept up his Greek and Latin, and tried his hand at German and drawing. It was not until his third year at Edinburgh that he followed Stewart's own course on political economy. Stewart's own reputation was that of an advanced Whig, and although he studiously avoided discussing politics with his young pupils, especially those who boarded with him, the tenets which underlay his political economy were radical by eighteenth-century standards. He lectured on population, national wealth, the poor law, the police and education. In his lectures on

national wealth he followed Adam Smith's ideas on free trade very closely
and he believed that 'the public happiness' depended more upon economic
factors than upon constitutions and political theory. Harry was fascinated
and took copious notes. The story that Sir William Hamilton's edition of
Stewart's works is based on Palmerston's notes is untrue but he was
certainly consulted about it in 1853 and expressed the view that Stewart's
opinions 'being founded on Truth' would not have become out of date.[10]
Adam Smith's views, as transmitted by Stewart, underlay most of
Palmerston's later thinking on economic questions and he frequently
referred to them in speeches and despatches.

Harry spent three years in Edinburgh but during his second year there his
father died. The disease, which was probably cancer of the throat,
progressed rapidly. Early in April 1802, Harry was sent for and came south
with his friend, Gilbert Elliot. Lord Palmerston died before his son
arrived. Lord Minto planned to break the news as gently as possible but,
unluckily, a servant, who did not know either young man by sight, mistook
Harry for Gilbert Elliot and blurted out the fact without warning. The
Palmerstons had always been a close-knit family and his father's
unexpected death shocked Harry deeply. Within three years his mother too
was dead. After her husband's death she plunged into a yet more feverish
social whirl which led John Ward to conclude uncharitably that she was
trying to marry off her 'ugly daughter', Frances. It probably had more to
do with her discovery, which she tried to keep from her son, that she too
was suffering from terminal cancer. She retired to Broadlands in May 1804
and died in January 1805.

His father's death caused practical problems for the new Viscount
Palmerston. He was not yet twenty-one and so could not assume
responsibility for his own estates. The family finances were already in
difficulties. The 1798 rising in Ireland made it impossible for some time to
collect the Irish rents, which were the basis of their income. The war had
adversely affected the family investments. They had also lost money trying
to save Benjamin Mee. But the basic cause of the problem was the second
Viscount's extravagance and inability to live within his income. When his
son succeeded, the Hampshire properties were mortgaged to the tune of
£10,000. Assets in hand could be reckoned at about £75,000 but liabilities,
including legacies, amounted to about £90,000. The legacies included sums
due to Lady Palmerston under her marriage jointure and substantial sums
set aside for the younger children. They also included provision for at least
one illegitimate son, Henry Campbell. Henry was well known to Harry,
although he may not previously have realized their exact relationship, but

he carried the matter off in style, writing a letter to Henry beginning, 'My dear Brother'. It was reckoned that, when all the most pressing claims had been attended to, the estate would for a time yield an unencumbered income of about £3,500 a year, of which £1,000 could reasonably be devoted to Harry's own education and maintenance.[11] It was hardly destitution but it left no room for extravagance.

His father had appointed trustees to look after his son's interests until he came of age. The most important of these was James Harris, first Earl of Malmesbury, who became in effect Palmerston's guardian. Although Malmesbury was now in semi-retirement, forced on him by increasing deafness, he had been recognized as one of England's greatest diplomats during his missions to the Prussia of Frederick the Great, the Russia of Catherine the Great, and The Hague. He took a close interest in Palmerston's career and the fact that the second Viscount chose him for the role may suggest that the elder Palmerston was still hoping his sons would follow a diplomatic career.

The most pressing question was the completion of Palmerston's education. It had been intended that he should go up to Cambridge in 1802 but, partly because of the financial problems, it was decided that he should spend another year in Edinburgh and postpone going to Cambridge, where the temptations to extravagance would be greater, until 1803. Two Cambridge colleges were particularly fashionable at that time, St John's and Trinity. Malmesbury favoured St John's where two of Palmerston's Harrow contemporaries, Haddo and Frederick Robinson, were already installed. Robinson persuaded Palmerston to join them – and Palmerston was also influenced by the information that St John's was more tolerant than Trinity about its undergraduates keeping horses.

It was taken for granted by Palmerston's guardians that the serious academic part of Palmerston's education was over when he left Edinburgh. At Cambridge it was the social life which counted. A nobleman was not permitted, let alone compelled, to sit the university examinations. Nevertheless, Palmerston still took both his classical and his mathematical studies quite seriously and voluntarily sat the twice-yearly college examinations at St John's. These were oral but classified and Palmerston was consistently placed in the first class even when he missed part of the term because of his mother's death.

There was still a sober side to Palmerston's character but perhaps his determination to study also represented his overflowing energy and his dislike of doing nothing. He also threw himself into drilling with the Volunteers who had been formed in anticipation of a French invasion after the breakdown of the Peace of Amiens. On his way south from Edinburgh in the summer of 1803 Palmerston himself had been caught up in a false alarm at Doncaster, when the beacons were lit as a warning that the French had landed. It is possible that Palmerston had already served with a hastily-organized and unrecognized volunteer group in Edinburgh. In Cambridge he was quickly promoted to be an officer. The university authorities looked with some suspicion on these undergraduate volunteers, whom they thought likely to get up to all sorts of mischief, but there was little they could do since they had official approval. Malmesbury thought it a splendid idea. Palmerston thoroughly enjoyed himself and remained keenly interested in militia and volunteer movements all his life.

By this time Palmerston had also found an active social life in Cambridge. Among his closest friends were Lawrence Sulivan, who subsequently married his sister Elizabeth, George Shee and Edward Clive, the grandson of Clive of India. All three became members of a very exclusive debating club, officially called the 'Speculative' but nicknamed (possibly by Palmerston) the 'Fusty'. Henry Goulburn was another member. Other men whose lives were to be closely linked with that of Palmerston, including Stratford Canning, Lord Ellenborough and John Cam Hobhouse, were also prominent members of the society, although not during Palmerston's time in Cambridge. The subjects debated were usually political and the society was regarded with some nervousness by the university but it was not suppressed; after all the two English universities were the recognized training grounds for aristocratic young politicians. Just how closely the two worlds were linked was brought home to Palmerston in January 1806 when the Prime Minister, William Pitt, who was also one of the two Cambridge university MPs, suddenly died.

3

Political Apprenticeship

The death of the Younger Pitt threw British politics into confusion, for in most people's eyes he was the only effective war leader against the French, the only man who could unite the Tories and most of the Whigs in the face of the national danger. The war situation already looked very bleak. Napoleon had defeated the Russians and the Austrians at Austerlitz in December 1805 and the Third Coalition had dissolved. Lord Grenville salvaged what he could, forming the so-called Ministry of All the Talents, which was actually a rather narrow, predominantly Foxite administration with Charles James Fox himself as Foreign Secretary. Although Fox had been a close friend of the second Viscount Palmerston, their political views had long since diverged and the elder Palmerston had moved towards that hostility to the French Revolution voiced by his other old friend, Edmund Burke.

Of more immediate interest to the younger Palmerston was the fact that Pitt's death necessitated a by-election for the vacant Cambridge university seat and he was persuaded by some of his St John's friends to stand. It was a forlorn hope. The seat was won, as expected, by the man who had preceded Palmerston at Dugald Stewart's hospitable home in Edinburgh, Lord Henry Petty, later Lord Lansdowne, who had already accepted office as Chancellor of the Exchequer in Grenville's administration. His friends hoped that Palmerston would at least beat his Harrow contemporary, Lord Althorpe, later Lord Spencer. In fact the final figures read – Petty, 331; Althorpe, 145; Palmerston, 128.

Palmerston stood again for the university seat in the general election of 1807. Political circumstances had changed by then. Grenville had been replaced as prime minister by the Duke of Portland, who had tried to reconstitute the Pittite coalition, and Palmerston had official backing but he still failed by three votes. Palmerston was inclined to blame his supposed running mate, Sir Vicary Gibbs, whom he described as 'almost as dangerous as my opponents'. To win both seats in a two-member constituency, where many electors were not voting a straight party ticket, required very careful management and there seem to have been elementary failures of tactics. Many of Gibbs' supporters 'plumped' for their man, that is cast only one vote, and did not, as they were expected to, give their second vote to Palmerston. The easy winner was Lord Euston, the son of the Duke of Grafton who was at that time the Chancellor of the University, but the second place went to Gibbs. It was perhaps some consolation to Palmerston that Petty did even worse.

Inexperience and poor organization contributed to Palmerston's failure but issues also played a part, the two most important being the abolition of the slave trade and Catholic Emancipation. The one great achievement of the Ministry of All the Talents was the abolition of the slave trade. Petty was known to be a strong supporter of the measure; Palmerston, ironically in view of his later exertions in the cause, was suspected of being hostile. But Catholic Emancipation was the key question. In 1801 the separate Irish parliament had been abolished. Ireland had been incorporated in the United Kingdom sending its MPs to Westminster. William Pitt had intended that the *quid pro quo* for this should be the removal of the most important civil disabilities from Roman Catholics, including those which prevented them from sitting in the Commons. George III had obstinately and consistently refused to countenance any such concessions which, he argued, would be contrary to his coronation oath to uphold the Protestant faith. The prejudices of the two English universities were with the king on this and it was therefore brave of Palmerston to let it be known that his own views were inclining to the other side.

Palmerston had at least advertised that he was interested in entering upon a political career and the patronage of Lord Malmesbury secured for him his first official appointment, as one of the six Junior Lords of the Admiralty, in the spring of 1807, even before he gained a parliamentary seat. It was not an onerous job. Palmerston himself said that he had to do little except sign his name to formal documents when required but it was a usual appointment for a beginner.

He had already made one other unsuccessful attempt to enter the Commons. In 1806 he stood for Horsham in Sussex. Horsham was a burgage borough with only 73 electors and for the best part of the previous century it had been regarded as a pocket borough by the Irwin family. The Irwin family interest had, however, recently been challenged by the Duke of Norfolk from his neighbouring seat at Arundel Castle. In 1806 Malmesbury drove a bargain with the current head of the Irwin family, Viscountess Irwin, that Palmerston and his own son, Lord Edward Fitzharris, should each pay her £1,500 for nomination as candidates and a further £3,500 each if they were elected and their return upheld, if necessary, on petition to the House of Commons. The last was a wise proviso. At the end of the election it was announced that the Duke of Norfolk's candidates had received 44 votes to their opponents' 29. Lady Irwin's agent challenged the qualification of most of Norfolk's supporters and maintained that his men had won by 29 to 15. The matter was remitted to the House of Commons, which eventually found for the Duke of Norfolk. Palmerston had paid £1,500 for nothing.

His next attempt to secure election for a pocket borough was more successful. His father had once sat for Newport in the Isle of Wight. Its patron, Sir Leonard Holmes, was prepared for the third Viscount to occupy it but on conditions. Palmerston himself recorded in his fragment of Autobiography published by Bulwer, 'One condition required of me, was that I should never, even for the election, set foot in the place; so jealous was the patron lest any attempt should be made to get a new interest in the borough.'[1]

Palmerston took his seat for the first time in the House of Commons in June 1807 as a Tory, or at least a Pittite, but he did not make his maiden speech until February 1808 when he defended the government's policy in attacking the Danish fleet at Copenhagen the previous September. It was a suitable topic for a Lord of the Admiralty, however junior, to speak upon and it was also popular. Some members protested that it had been improper for the navy to attack the Danes, who were still neutral, but George Canning, the Foreign Secretary, made short work of that by revealing that the government had had secret information (correct as it happened) that the French were on the point of seizing the Danish fleet.

Palmerston's own speech was a qualified success. It lasted about half an hour. Bulwer said of it that those parts which Palmerston had memorized were spoken with ease and felicity but when he tried to speak *ex tempore,* 'there was that hesitation and superabundance of gesture with the hands, which were perceptible to the last when Lord Palmerston spoke unprepared, and was seeking for words; for though he always used the right word, it often cost him pains to find it'.[2] Although Palmerston told his sister, Elizabeth, that he had not felt so 'alarmed' as he expected and although everybody was very complimentary about it, he was obviously not very satisfied with it himself and he did not speak again that session.

Instead he began to turn his attention to his Irish estates which he visited for the first time with his brother, William, in September 1808. It was fairly dismaying. He told Elizabeth, 'There is a great deal, I may almost say, everything to be done and it will be absolutely necessary for me to repeat my visit next summer and probably make it annual for some time to come.' The main estate, north of Sligo, lay in a 'tract of country about two miles broad and six miles long, bounded on one side by the sea, and on the other by bog and high, craggy mountains. It is wholly unimproved.' Nevertheless, Palmerston thought that with time and patience the bog could be brought under cultivation and the arable made three times as valuable. He thought it even more urgent to repair the parish church 'so as to make it fit for service', to build roads, and to establish schools. The people were anxious for education and he had plans to build three good school houses on his estate, each with three or four acres of land on which the schoolmaster could keep a cow and grow potatoes. He would not starve therefore, if his pupils provided him with insufficient fees. It would also make him Palmerston's tenant and he could turn him off at will if he proved unsatisfactory. He supposed, however, that the schoolmasters would have to be Catholics 'for the people will not send their children to a Protestant'. As a further measure of education, Palmerston intended to introduce 'a Scotch farmer' to teach the people to improve their land. He also had ambitious plans for establishing a 'little manufacturing village' and building a pier and making a port 'near a village that stands on a point of land projecting into Donegal Bay, and called Mullaghmore'. But the biggest problem of all was that the land had been continually sub-divided until many tenants had holdings much too small to be farmed economically – sometimes only four or five acres – but they could not be turned off because they had no other means of subsistence. The problem was compounded by the activities of the middle men, or 'petty landlords', who sub-let small plots to under-tenants and charged them sufficient both to cover the middle man's own rent and make a profit for him. Palmerston determined to get rid of these middle men wherever possible.[3]

Not much, however, could be accomplished in one short visit and Palmerston was soon back in England where the main political action lay. In September 1809 George Canning, the Foreign Secretary, and Lord Castlereagh, the Secretary of State for War, fought their famous duel, which arose out of Castlereagh's suspicions that Canning was trying to saddle him with the entire responsibility for the disastrous failure of the Walcheren expedition. The quarrel brought down Portland's administration and Spencer Perceval became Prime Minister.

Perceval summoned Palmerston from Broadlands and offered him the Chancellorship of the Exchequer. This was not yet the great office of state it has since become. The Chancellor was then essentially an assistant to the Prime Minister in his official capacity as First Lord of the Treasury and Perceval promised Palmerston that he, Perceval, would still 'take the principal share of the Treasury business, both in and out of the House'. Palmerston was not more inexperienced than Henry Petty had been when he became Grenville's Chancellor and his family connections with the City of London and his known interest in political economy must have made the Exchequer look like a natural career direction at that time. Nevertheless, it was a bold offer to a young and untried man, and Perceval more or less admitted to Palmerston that he was at his wit's end how to fill the post. It seemed unlikely that the government would last for long but that was not the main reason for Palmerston's hesitation. He told Perceval that he was afraid he would find himself 'wholly incompetent . . . both from my inexperience in the details of matters of Finance & my want of practice in public speaking'. More experienced men might be able to carry him in the actual conduct of business but he would have to defend the government's policy in the Commons in what promised to be a particularly difficult session. Palmerston had not established himself as a speaker – he had not spoken at all since his rather mediocre maiden speech – and he feared to make a fool of himself and damn his political career before it had really started. He told Malmesbury, 'It is throwing for a *great stake* & where much may be gained, very much also is to be lost.' Malmesbury, tactfully but firmly, endorsed all Palmerston's own misgivings.[4]

Perceval seems to have realized from the beginning that Palmerston was not very likely to accept and was ready with a number of alternative suggestions. Possibly Palmerston might come in as a Junior Lord of the Treasury, an equivalent post to the one he already had at the Admiralty, and take the Chancellorship when he had a little more experience of finance, or he might take another post entirely as Secretary at War.

Palmerston opted for the job of Secretary at War, as being 'one better suited to a beginner'. The phrase caused Guedalla a good deal of amusement since, as he pointed out, Britain was 'engaged at the moment in a war with Napoleon'.[5] But it was not quite such an absurd estimate of the situation as it sounded. The Secretary at War was a second-rank appointment. The head of the War Office was the Secretary for War and the Colonies. The Secretary at War had a position very roughly equivalent to that of a Minister of State in a modern government department with, in theory, a clearly defined area of responsibility. The post, unlike the

Chancellorship of the Exchequer, did not normally carry a place in the Cabinet, although there were occasional precedents for it doing so, and Perceval in fact offered it. Palmerston turned it down against Malmesbury's advice. Again he seems to have feared being too conspicuous and ruining his future career if either he blundered or the administration came to grief. He told Malmesbury that he would have plenty to do learning the business of the War Office without Cabinet responsibilities. Such extreme caution is very unlike the later Palmerston but it seems to have been characteristic of the young man.

The Secretaryship at War was certainly enough to be going on with. In theory the division of responsibilities within the administration of the army was rational. Paying for the army lay within the prerogatives of parliament. Army finance therefore came under a minister, the Secretary at War, who could answer for it in parliament. Army discipline and promotion had originally come under the prerogative of the crown. They were therefore in the hands of the Commander-in-Chief, who was not a parliamentary figure and had his headquarters at the Horse Guards. In practice, it had never been possible to lay down exact boundaries of jurisdiction between the War Office and the Horse Guards. Over the years, every kind of anomaly and special case had developed. The artillery, for example, came under the Board of Ordnance in Palace Yard, rather than under the Horse Guards. It was extraordinarily difficult to find out who was responsible for supplies and various aspects of the commissariat − a fact which bedevilled the British army from the American War of Independence to the Crimea. The Treasury, and even the Home Office, also had certain, usually ill-defined, responsibilities. As a result of historical accidents, the Secretary at War had to deal with all sorts of non-financial problems, like the trial of deserters. No one was sure where any of the boundaries lay and everyone defended his territory, or supposed territory, with the grim determination appropriate to a military department. Philip Guedalla found the details of the quarrels in which Palmerston became involved irresistibly funny and presented the picture as a black comedy, played out against the backdrop of the Napoleonic wars.

But the serious issues which lay behind the peculiar details were clear enough to Palmerston and his contemporaries. This was the reign of George III and the boundaries between parliamentary and royal prerogatives were still fluid. Equally difficult was the fact that new standards of public integrity were battling against older more casual attitudes. At this time the Commander-in-Chief was usually a royal Duke.

Until 1809 it had been the king's brother, the Duke of York, but he had to retire temporarily as the result of an embarrassing scandal when his mistress, Mrs Clark, was found to have been selling army commissions. His place was taken by General Sir David Dundas. Dundas's own story of his humble origins – that as the son of a small Edinburgh tradesman he had walked to London and bought a commission with borrowed money – seems a little overdrawn in view of the fact that his uncle was a general, but he was a man who had risen largely by his own exertions and he was devoted to his patron, the Duke of York. He was determined that during his temporary incumbency of the Commander-in-Chief's post – until it was deemed suitable for York to return in 1811 – he would give up no jot or tittle of the prerogatives of the office.

The first quarrel between Palmerston and Dundas turned on a typically eighteenth-century point. The distinction between a man's private fortune and public money entrusted to him for some official purpose was by no means clear. This was particularly true in the service departments. The famous impeachment of Lord Melville (himself distantly related to Sir David Dundas) a few years earlier had hinged on the fact that, as Secretary of the Navy, Melville had been careless in keeping his accounts separate. In the army the matter was complicated by the fact that historically a wealthy man would be 'commissioned' to raise a regiment in return for a lump sum. Whether he used his private fortune for the public service, or made a profit, depended on circumstances and his own astuteness. Since many public servants were not paid a salary at all commensurate with their responsibilities, the assumption was that they would take the rest in perquisites. It was a system which dated back to Tudor times and earlier. The first serious attempts to change it were made in the late-eighteenth century and Palmerston and his protagonists were caught up in the transition between the two systems.

In the autumn of 1809 Dundas asked the new Secretary at War to sign a warrant appointing Dundas's father-in-law, General De Lancey, a Commissioner for governing Chelsea Hospital. Unfortunately, an enquiry in 1806 had established that De Lancey, when Barrack-Master-General from 1793 to 1804, had been transferring money from the public to his private purse at a rate which was considered excessive even by the standards of the time. (De Lancey admitted to being in possession of £6,856 of public money; the enquiry thought he had actually had at least £97,415). Palmerston was not as green as that and referred the matter to the Prime Minister, who vetoed the appointment.

Palmerston then moved to try to prevent generals from claiming allowances for ADC's who were not in fact on their staff. Dundas grudgingly admitted that the practice must cease. Palmerston ran into much more serious problems over the question of clothing allowances. Technically, clothing was allowed for in a private soldier's pay. In practice, the money was paid over to the colonel of the regiment who was responsible for the provision of the clothing. Palmerston felt that proof ought to be forthcoming that the sums allocated had in fact been expended on clothing of the proper quality. For Dundas, this was going much too far. He accused Palmerston of arrogance and raised a much more serious issue when he asserted that the Secretary at War was, by the terms of his commission, subordinate to, and subject to the orders of, the Commander-in-Chief. Palmerston sent the Prime Minister an immensely long memorandum tracing the history of both appointments back even before 1688 to prove that this had never been so.

There was the germ of a major constitutional crisis in the question. The matter was referred to the King, or in practice to the Prince Regent since George III was now incapable of transacting business. The Prince hastily referred it back to the Prime Minister, Spencer Perceval, who decided in principle for Palmerston. The Secretary at War was not subordinate to the Commander-in-Chief. But it was a qualified victory because he advised the young man in future to consult the Commander-in-Chief before taking decisions which impinged on army practice. Bulwer's summing up still seems judicious. He wrote, 'This, in fact, solved none of the questions which had been raised; but it prevented the entire subordination of the civil authority to the military one'.[6]

Palmerston also addressed himself to the re-organization of the War Office itself. It had naturally swollen in numbers – although by modern standards modestly – as a result of the war. Its staff rose from 51 in 1797 to 144 in 1810. Its organization was chaotic. An enquiry in 1809, before Palmerston arrived, suggested some rationalization and economies, which Palmerston tried to enforce in 1810. Once the war was over and the post-1815 depression began, a Select Committee in 1817 called for reductions in public expenditure and a slimming down of the War Office. Reductions in numbers were made between 1820 and 1822. Although Palmerston tried to be generous in the matter of pensions, a good deal of resentment was generated. Recruitment was still by personal recommendation and Palmerston attempted to introduce at least a basic probationary period, which enabled the Office to dispense with a man after two months if he proved quite unsuitable. He also tried to replace promotion by seniority with promotion by merit. This too caused resentment and Palmerston was honest enough to admit privately that 'merit' tended to mean the promotion of those he liked, in particular he employed and quickly promoted his brother-in-law, Henry Sulivan.

Nepotism was still endemic throughout the British civil service and dissatisfied clerks leaked details of the most scandalous cases to the press. Palmerston also tightened up the organization of the Office, insisting that the clerks worked the six-hour day (Saturdays included) that they were supposed to, and that papers were properly signed and accounted for – previously it had been almost impossible to find anything in the War Office. Even his critics admitted that Palmerston worked very hard himself and Bourne seems justified in concluding that at this time Palmerston emerges as something of a bureaucrat.[7] He was certainly unpopular with many people and Mrs Arbuthnot's well-known comment when he left office in May 1828, that the clerks would have illuminated the windows as for a military victory if they had dared, was probably correct.

One dissatisfied man took even more drastic action in 1818. A Lieutenant Davies, a retired officer on the half-pay list, 'maddened perhaps by correspondence with the War Department' about his pension[8] – shot at him as he ascended the steps to his office. Only Palmerston's habit of running upstairs saved him. As it was he was badly bruised by a glancing blow near his spine. There were fears at the time, amid the general unrest of the post-war depression, that this was an attempt at a political assassination but it seems to have been the act of a single madman.

Palmerston's main public duty as Secretary at War was to move the annual army estimates in the Commons. All agreed that he did this in an efficient and workmanlike manner. He was audible and understood his figures. His private papers show that he did a great deal of work to prepare himself to meet parliamentary attacks. His two most formidable antagonists were Henry Brougham, with whom he had quarrels which seem to date back to Edinburgh days, and the radical Joseph Hume, whose attacks were more clearly politically motivated. Palmerston found himself in the unenviable position of having annually to defend the practice of flogging in the British army, although he was becoming privately convinced that it was indefensible. The most he could do was to try to get the maximum sentence reduced from 500 to 200 lashes.

Palmerston was establishing a reputation for efficiency but nothing more. Some of his friends were disappointed. When he first moved the army estimates in 1810 Lady Minto wrote to her husband, then in India, 'He will never boast of shining talents, or great views, but he is painstaking, & gentlemanlike to the greatest degree, & will always swim where greater talents might sink.' Lady Malmesbury was also critical. She wrote, 'On such subjects where clearness & perspicacity are the requisites & time is given for preparation, he will always succeed, but where *opinions* are to be given & *effect to be produced* by *spontaneous* eloquence I doubt it. He is *reserved* & so *very cautious,* so *singularly* so for a young man, so afraid of *committing himself* even in common life & conversation with his most intimate friends, that it will throw a coldness & want of effect on such speeches of his.'[9] As the years went by Palmerston gained more confidence and was prepared to retaliate on his opponents but his retorts seem to have frequently misfired. He was accused of being 'flippant' and of 'sneering'. Admittedly, the severest criticisms came from his political enemies but even those who were sympathetic felt that he often misjudged the mood of the House and threw away his advantage over Hume by being unnecessarily insulting.

Despite his rather mediocre Commons performance, it is surprising that Palmerston remained in the comparatively junior office of Secretary at War from 1809 to 1828. Particularly after the Napoleonic wars came to an end in 1815, it was something of a hack job. Palmerston had had other offers. In 1812 Spencer Perceval was assassinated and Lord Liverpool, the new Prime Minister, suggested that Palmerston might become Secretary for Ireland. Palmerston was now taking an enthusiastic, if rather intermittent, interest in the development of his Irish estates but the offer did not attract him. In 1826 Palmerston was offered the Presidency of the Board of Control for India, with the promise of the Governor-Generalship of India when it became vacant, but he declined it. About the same time he was offered the Postmaster Generalship with a peerage. The offer had already been made, more tentatively, in 1822 but on both occasions he refused it. Palmerston was to remain a House of Commons man to the end of his days.

If Palmerston was an ambitious man, as his letters to Malmesbury in 1809 seemed to indicate, his career was plainly not developing very satisfactorily. Politically he was rather isolated. Palmerston's personal friends at this time were not 'political friends': his only real intimates were Henry Sulivan and George Shee who were not influential. His political connections were with the Tories but his social connections were with the Whigs. As Bulwer puts it, 'He certainly was not a Whig, and yet he lived chiefly in Whig society which, since the time of Mr Fox, was the society most in fashion.'[10]

He supported the repressive legislation passed after 1815 to counter the growing political and economic discontent, went out of his way to support the magistrates' actions at Peterloo and, in his capacity as Secretary at War, emphasized the need for the government to have sufficient troops at its disposal to meet challenges like Peterloo or the attempt by a group of extreme radicals to set up a provisional government in Glasgow in 1820. With memories of the role of the National Guard in the French Revolution he urged that barracks be built so that the troops would not mingle with, and perhaps be tempted to side with, the populace.

Only on Catholic Emancipation did Palmerston step out of line with Tory policy. He supported Grattan's motion in 1813 to set up a Committee to consider the question. The arguments he advanced were hardly radical. He refused to concede that Catholics had any right to demand admission to certain offices but argued rather that it was foolish of the state to deny itself their services, pointing out how unfortunate it would have been if Nelson or Wellington had happened to be born a Catholic.[11]

His firmness on the Catholic issue is the more remarkable because it was an embarrassment to him in his attempts to win the Cambridge University seat, which he was still determined to do. He nursed the university constituency assiduously, going there frequently to socialize and making a point of appointing St John's men to army chaplaincies – among other oddities, the Secretary at War was responsible for such appointments. His chance came in 1811 when the Duke of Grafton died and Lord Eustace's succession to the peerage caused a by-election. Although he canvassed most assiduously, he was pessimistic about his chances because of the Catholic question. In fact he was elected. He retained the seat until 1831, although he was challenged in 1826 by fellow Tories, also on the Catholic issue, and was so angered by the tepid support that he received from Liverpool on that occasion, that he warned him he would not remain in the government, if he lost the Cambridge seat.

By this time Palmerston was heavily involved in matters outside politics. From 1808 onwards he made serious attempts to improve his Irish estates, usually going there annually in September to check on the progress of his improvements. By 1826 he could tell his brother, William, that the harbour on Donegal Bay was almost complete and that, if he could persuade people to build a (horse-drawn) railroad to it from Loch Erne, it would link up with the inland navigation system and handle the exports and imports of a large and fertile area. He was slowly reclaiming his own bogs, hopefully at a rate of sixty acres a year, but it was a laborious process and he seems to have had more hope of developing simple industry. He established 'an infant linen market' at Cliffony and a lime kiln nearby, from which he could undersell his competitors.[12]

The spur was his own financial difficulties. He never recovered from the debts his father had left him. He sold the house at East Sheen in 1806 and had to increase the mortgage on Broadlands to £14,000 in 1817. He was notorious for not paying his bills, especially to tradesmen. There is a well-known story of how one butcher forced his way into Palmerston's presence and compelled him to sign a cheque. Palmerston then ostentatiously threw the polluted pen out of the window. But this was untypical. Usually he waited to be sued. He lost eighteen such actions – generally for sums varying between £300 and £2 – between 1811 and 1841 and settled a nineteenth out of court.[13]

He tried his hand at investments both for himself and for his brother, William. His father had acquired lime works at Fairburn in Yorkshire and slate quarries at Tan-y-bwlch in Caernarfonshire. Palmerston set out to develop both and even formed a company, the Welsh Slate Company, to develop the quarries. The Welsh Slate Company eventually became prosperous but at first it was a considerable drain. By 1830 he had invested £10,000 without return. From 1828 onwards he regularly visited Tan-y-bwlch on his way back from Ireland and had rather grandiose schemes for railway and tunnel projects. He also thought of linking it with his Sligo ventures by shipping out the slates for his buildings there. The quarries began to pay modest, if intermittent, dividends in the 1830s and by the 1860s he was receiving annual dividends of over £9,000.

It was, however, his only successful venture. In other companies such as the Welsh Iron and Coal Company, the Norfolk Railway, a Pearl Fishery Company and the Pesco-Peruvian Company, he was lucky if he recovered his initial investment. But the Company which ended in serious embarrassment was the Devon and Cornwall Mining Company, of which he had been persuaded to become a Director in 1825. After the shares plunged alarmingly, the Directors were accused in a petition to Parliament of having acted fraudulently. Palmerston told the Commons that he had had nothing to do with the formation of the Company and had himself lost heavily by it but it is possible that the scandal cost him the Chancellorship of the Exchequer in 1827.[14]

Palmerston's own life-style was expensive. He does not seem to have had his father's interest in art, the theatre or scientific discoveries. He did, however, spend a certain amount on further improvements at Broadlands and, more particularly, on the gardens. Despite his lack of interest in gambling, he also invested in racehorses on a large scale always hoping that his winnings would at least cover his outlay but they never did. His social life was as frenetic as that of his parents. In spite of his hard work at the

War Office, he found time to attend balls, sailing parties, shooting parties and every other kind of social event. He belonged to all the obvious clubs, White's, the Travellers and the Athenaeum among them. He also belonged to Almack's, the most exclusive club in London, admission to which was carefully controlled by the seven Lady Patronesses. Palmerston was elected without difficulty. It was popularly supposed that no fewer than three of the Patronesses, Lady Cowper, Lady Jersey and Countess (later Princess) Lieven, had been his mistresses. Lady Jersey probably was. Countess Lieven, the wife of the Russian ambassador, was so inclined to claim that she had made a conquest of every influential man in Europe (she was certainly the mistress of Metternich and of Guizot) that it is difficult to know the truth but Palmerston probably escaped her clutches.

Of the three, it was Lady Cowper who was consistently important in Palmerston's life. Born Emily Lamb, the sister of William Lamb, later Lord Melbourne, Victoria's first Prime Minister, she had known Harry Temple from childhood. In 1805, at the age of eighteen, she married Earl Cowper. She enjoyed the position it gave her in society but she found her husband unbearably dull. She probably first became Palmerston's mistress in 1809. They were faithful to each other in their own fashion — which is to say entirely unfaithful — until Cowper's death in 1837 made it possible for her to marry Palmerston in 1839. Three of Emily's children, Emily (Minnie), William and Frances, were probably Palmerston's although Emily was known, or believed, to have had many other lovers, including Francis Conyngham, the son of George IV's mistress, Lady Conyngham, the mysterious Count Guiliano, the Corsican diplomat Pozzo di Borgo, and Count Flahault, supposedly the son of Talleyrand. Palmerston became angrily jealous on a number of occasions. But he himself had many other mistresses. Sometimes he laid himself open to blackmail as with Mrs Murray Mills, who had acted under the name of Emma Mills, and by whom Palmerston had a son, Henry John, in 1816. Professor Bourne's revelations from Palmerston's diaries show how many brief affairs he had. In a very transparent code he meticulously recorded both his successes and failures — his father had kept a similar diary.[15]

His friends seem to have expected Palmerston to marry on a number of occasions from 1809 onwards. He did not do so, rejoicing rather in the nickname of 'Lord Cupid', which either the press or Lady Jersey, had bestowed upon him. But there are indications that he was not really the jaunty Palmerston of later legend. His career was not going particularly well. He was in deep financial trouble. He was in love with a woman he could not marry and on whose loyalty he could not rely. He consoled himself with the feverish pursuit of other women. In 1828, at the age of forty-four, he had achieved little and seemed destined, like his father, to be a minor politician and, even as a social figure, less known and less respected than his father had been.

4

The Canningite?

Palmerston was shaken loose from his niche as a minor Tory politician in 1827 by the illness and subsequent death of the Prime Minister, Lord Liverpool. In April 1827 the Foreign Secretary, George Canning, agreed to try to form a ministry. Once again he offered Palmerston the Chancellorship of the Exchequer and a seat in the Cabinet. This time Palmerston accepted but there were complications. It was necessary for any minister changing offices to seek re-election and a by-election was already pending in the other Cambridge University seat because John Copley had gone to the Lords as Baron Lyndhurst on becoming Lord Chancellor. Since it was thought risky for Palmerston to defend his seat at the same time, it was agreed that Canning, as Prime Minister, would keep the Chancellorship of the Exchequer in his own hands and Palmerston remain at the War Office until the end of the parliamentary session.

But, apart from the Devon Mining Company scandal, it became apparent that the King, George IV, was hostile to Palmerston and wanted a nominee of his own, George Herries, at the Exchequer. Canning broke the news to Palmerston in a very embarrassed interview in which he offered Palmerston the governorship of Jamaica instead. Palmerston laughed uproariously until he realized that Canning was serious. A little later Canning offered him the Governor-Generalship of India. Palmerston took this rather more seriously but declined. He told Canning in phrases redolent of the eighteenth century, 'I felt what means it afforded for increasing one's fortune, for gratifying one's love of power, for affording a scope for doing good upon a magnificent theatre of action; but my ambition was satisfied with my position at home. I happened not to have a family for whom I should be desirous of providing, and my health would not stand the climate of India.'[1] He stayed at the War Office where things were more peaceful than usual because, since the death of the Duke of York in January 1827, he had been exercising the functions of Commander-in-Chief, as well as Secretary at War.

Palmerston was often later described as a pupil of Canning and it was a description which he occasionally adopted himself when it suited him but in many ways it is more misleading than helpful. He had known Canning, who was fifteen years his senior, since as a younger man he had moved in the same literary and social circles. When Canning first went to the Foreign Office in 1807, it had been suggested that he might take Palmerston as his Under-Secretary but he had preferred Charles Bagot. In fact, during his early days in office, Palmerston had been more associated with Plumer Ward and the anti-Canning faction. But, after 1822, his support for the cause of Catholic emancipation had put him on the side of Canning against the ultra-Tories, the 'pig-tailed Tories' as Palmerston himself nicknamed them. The fact that he remained in office with Canning in 1827 when Wellington, Bathurst, Robert Peel and others disassociated themselves from the ministry, grouped him firmly with the Canningites.

Although Palmerston never became Chancellor of the Exchequer, he had taken his seat in the Cabinet in April 1827. For the first time he saw the full range of cabinet papers, including those relating to foreign affairs. This seems to have sparked a new interest in him. He had rarely spoken on foreign affairs – although he did make a spirited defence of the British empire when he presented the army estimates in 1816, but that was mainly to justify keeping up a larger peacetime establishment than his critics thought necessary.[2] Generally, his interests at the War Office had been limited and technical. It was his brother, William, who had fulfilled their father's hopes by going into the diplomatic service. In 1827 Palmerston secured for him the post of Secretary of Embassy in the Russian capital of St Petersburg. Since the newly appointed Ambassador, Sir William A'Court, later Lord Heytesbury, could not take up his appointment immediately, William became chargé d'affaires. The two Temple brothers were beginning to gravitate towards high diplomacy.

Canning's ministry lasted only a few months. In August the Prime Minister died. Although his friends had been alarmed by his appearance for some time, his final collapse was unexpected and the political world was in disarray. He was succeeded by a Harrow contemporary of Palmerston, Frederick Robinson, now Viscount Goderich. No one seriously supposed Goderich to be equal to the job and he resigned in January 1828 without meeting Parliament. Palmerston, although once again offered the Chancellorship of the Exchequer by Goderich, had stayed at his post at the War Office.

The King now sent for the Duke of Wellington. It was generally expected that Wellington would form a Tory and 'Protestant' administration of those who had refused to join Canning in 1827. In fact he tried to reconstruct Liverpool's long-lasting government. This involved bringing in the group who were now usually described as 'Canningites' – William Huskisson, the Secretary for War and the Colonies, Charles Grant, the President of the Board of Trade, Lord Dudley, the Foreign Secretary, and Palmerston himself. It was an uneasy coalition with much distrust on both sides, which only lasted until May 1828.

The first serious dispute was about the sliding scale to be applied to the Corn Duties. On this, Wellington compromised. The second was about the disfranchisement of Penrhyn and East Retford for electoral corruption. The Tories wanted the seats merged with the neighbouring 'hundreds', that is, country districts. The Canningites wanted the seats transferred to the large manufacturing cities of Manchester and Birmingham, which still had no separate representation. A compromise was reached by which the East Retford seat was to be given to Birmingham but the Penrhyn seat to the hundred. When the matter reached the floor of the House of Commons, however, a Tory backbencher moved an amendment that the East Retford seat should go to the neighbouring hundred of Bassetlaw. The Tory ministers voted for it, the Canningites against. Huskisson subsequently offered his resignation to Wellington, who accepted it. Even then, the Canningites were reluctant to go. Huskisson contended that his resignation had only been conditional and a compromise could still have been found. Palmerston sought out Wellington and had a long conversation with him, pacing up and down the gallery of the House of Lords, but it was Palmerston who did the arguing. Wellington was adamant and, in the end, the Canningites resigned as a party.

Their clinging to office struck even contemporaries as odd. On most important domestic issues they had ceased to agree with the government and were nearer to the Whigs. Their remaining in the ministry was undoubtedly influenced by their desire to continue Canning's policy in foreign affairs. The crucial man here was Lord Dudley, the Foreign Secretary. As an individual he was almost totally ineffective. He had become Foreign Secretary when Canning became Prime Minister. Canning would have preferred to have remained Foreign Secretary himself but, when he failed to promote Palmerston immediately to the Chancellorship of the Exchequer, he realized that he could not possibly hold all three posts simultaneously. Dudley took the Foreign Office on the extraordinary grounds that he had a 'curiosity . . . to have a peep at official life. In three

months I cannot do *much* harm to the publick, or to myself';[3] and prepared
to be Canning's mouthpiece. When they joined Wellington's ministry, the
Canningites insisted that Dudley stay in place, as the 'guarantee' that
Canning's policy would be continued, especially over Greece. Wellington
agreed to keep Dudley for the time being, although making the Chancellor
of the Duchy of Lancaster, the Earl of Aberdeen (Palmerston's Harrow
contemporary, Lord Haddo), Dudley's 'coadjutor' and nominated
successor – who in fact took over in May 1828.

The great foreign question of the moment was the Eastern crisis. The
break-up of the Ottoman empire was the most persistent and the most
serious international problem with which European diplomats had to deal
during the nineteenth century. They first became conscious of it towards
the end of the previous century when the Russia of Catherine the Great
advanced to the River Dniester and seized the Crimea from the Turks. The
interests of all the Great Powers, with the possible exception of Prussia,
were involved in the Eastern Mediterranean and it was realized that the
collapse of the Turkish empire would destabilize the whole of Europe. The
Eastern question involved Europe in war in 1854 and in 1914 and there were
narrow escapes in 1828 and 1878. In the 1820s the problem focused on
Greece.

The domination of Moslem Turkey over part of Christian Europe in the
Balkans was the most sensitive issue. In 1821 the 'Greeks' rose against the
Turks, first in the Danubian Provinces (now Roumania), then in the
Morea, the southern part of modern Greece. The movement was ill-
understood in the West. Western Philhellenes saw the rebels either as the
spiritual descendants of the Greeks of the time of Homer and of Pericles,
or as modern nationalists trying to establish a nation state. Those who
knew the area better realized that neither picture was correct. The binding
force was religion, membership of the Greek Orthodox Church, and the
original ambition was to take over the moribund Ottoman empire. The
Turks struck back savagely. The Greek Patriarch of Constantinople was
executed; the Greek population of cities like Smyrna, massacred. There
were atrocities on the Greek side too, particularly in the Morea, but they
were less known in Europe. Public sympathy, especially in France, tended
to be on the Greek side but this was not universally the case. Conservatives
saw it as suspicious that radicals who had been defeated in Germany, Italy
and Spain in the early 1820s went as volunteers to help the Greeks. But,
most of all, governments feared international complications and perhaps
even war.

In 1825 the Sultan Mahmud II persuaded his vassal, Mehemet Ali, Pasha of Egypt, to send his son, Ibrahim, with an army to re-conquer the Morea. The Tsar of Russia, Alexander I, contemplated intervention. When Alexander died towards the end of 1825, Canning sent the Duke of Wellington, nominally to offer formal congratulations to his successor, Nicholas, but mainly to obtain an agreement on Greece. In April 1826 the two Powers signed the Protocol of St Petersburg, which was converted into the Treaty of London the following year when the French adhered. The three Powers called for an immediate armistice and offered their mediation. The Greeks were to remain under the suzerainty of Turkey but to enjoy considerable autonomy in the conduct of their own affairs. The boundaries of the new state were to be determined later. The Greeks agreed to an armistice; the Turks did not and, as the result of a muddled series of events, an allied fleet of British, French and Russian warships sank a Turko-Egyptian fleet at Navarino Bay in October 1827.

Wellington, who became Prime Minister four months later, was aghast at this turn of events. He had no doubt that Russia was the real danger in the Eastern Mediterranean and that Britain must uphold the integrity of the Ottoman empire at all costs. Palmerston was convinced, rightly or wrongly, that Wellington's dislike of Russia was partly personal, stemming from what he had seen as discourteous treatment when he was in Russia in 1826 and his quarrels with the Russian Ambassador in London, Count Lieven and his formidable wife. Palmerston's own reaction was completely different. The Greek papers were some of the first he saw when he became a member of the Cabinet and he quickly made up his mind where he stood, not perhaps altogether appreciating the complexities of the situation. He concluded that Greece must be truly independent and with as extensive boundaries as possible, including Attica as well as the Morea. Peel agreed with him about the importance of independence and Aberdeen privately agreed with him that Attica, including Athens, should be part of the new Greece, even though it was not then in rebel hands. Palmerston knew of Peel's sympathy but he supposed Aberdeen to be entirely identified with Wellington's hard-line policy.[4] The five months the Canningites remained in Wellington's Cabinet was for Palmerston a time of complete frustration. Freed from the constraints of office, he vigorously attacked the government's policy the following year, when he condemned the absurdity of trying to set up a Greek state which should contain 'neither Athens nor Thebes, nor Marathon, nor Salamis, nor Plataea, nor Thermopylae, nor Missolonghi'.[5] Byron had died at Missolonghi in 1824 but the other names, evocative of classical Greece, reveal Palmerston as the typical western Philhellene.

A change in policy was forced on Wellington by external events. In April 1828 Russia went to war with Turkey, nominally about shipping rights in the Bosporus and not about Greece at all, but it was soon clear that the settlement in Greece would be mainly determined by the outcome of the war. The Russians alarmed the other Powers by apparently reclaiming the right to act entirely in their own interests, unfettered by the Treaty of London. New diplomatic formulae were found but Wellington felt compelled to agree to the despatch of a French army to the Morea, a move he had previously resisted. The Russians, after some initial reverses, decisively defeated the Turks and compelled them to accept the Treaty of Adrianople (1829). This gave the Russians further territory on the eastern side of the Black Sea and a quasi-protectorate over the Danubian Principalities of Moldavia and Wallachia.

The boundaries of Greece were finally settled in February 1830. Greece was to be, as Palmerston wished, fully independent. But, to reassure the Tsar, it was agreed that it should be a monarchy. Leopold of Saxe-Coburg, later Leopold of the Belgians, was offered the throne but declined it. The issue was still unsettled when Wellington's government fell. Palmerston in his first term at the Foreign Office played his part in determining that the new King should be Prince Otto of Bavaria. It was, he subsequently admitted, 'the worst day's work he ever did'. Otto, as a Roman Catholic, was automatically suspect to his Greek subjects, among whom religious feelings still ran very high. Worse still, he was only seventeen and surrounded by a clique of Bavarian officers, who knew and cared little about Greece. His government was to be overthrown by revolution in 1843, although Otto himself was not deposed until 1862.

Palmerston's reaction to the Greek problem in 1828 was generous but impulsive. The same was true of his attitude to Portugal where the situation was equally complicated. The Portuguese royal family had fled to their great overseas dependency, Brazil, in 1807 to escape from Napoleon. The King, John VI, did not return to Portugal until 1821. The following year he accepted a new constitution which abolished feudalism, limited the power of the Church and established parliamentary government. He had left his elder son, Pedro, as Regent in Brazil but his younger son, Miguel, allowed himself to be placed at the head of an army revolt against the new constitution. John took refuge on a British warship. Miguel was eventually compelled to submit and banished to Vienna. When John died in 1826 his son, Pedro, elected to stay in Brazil and relinquished the Portuguese throne to his seven year old daughter, Donna Maria Gloria, at the same time granting a new constitution, the 'Charter', to replace the 1822 constitution, which had been abrogated in the troubles of 1823. The right-wing army proclaimed Miguel King, contending that Pedro's abdication must cover his descendants as well as himself. Canning cared very little about the internal constitutional wrangles in Portugal – he rightly recognized that many of Maria's supporters were constitutionalists from expediency rather than conviction[6] – but, as in Greece, he did care about international complications. In 1823 he had made it clear that the French intervention in Spain, sanctioned by the Holy Alliance Powers of Russia, Austria and Prussia, to suppress the liberals there, must not be extended to Portugal. In 1827 he actually sent 5,000 British troops to support Maria. A compromise was reached by which Miguel was to marry his niece, Maria, and to act as Regent until she came of age. Miguel returned to Portugal about the time that Wellington's government assumed office in Britain.

It had been arranged that the British forces, both military and naval, should be withdrawn and this withdrawal was underway when it became obvious that Miguel was breaking the spirit, and eventually the letter, of the 1827 agreement. He dissolved the elected Chamber and summoned the old Portuguese parliament of the three Estates, the Cortes, which in June 1828 proclaimed him King. Maria fled to Brazil. Wellington's reaction was very different from that of Canning. Both men shared the same objective, a stable Portugal, which would be a good trading partner for Britain and not subject to the meddling of potentially hostile Powers, especially France. But Wellington believed that Miguel was acceptable to the majority of the Portuguese people, who acknowledged his right to become King on Pedro's abdication and whose instincts were conservative and monarchical, rather than liberal and parliamentary. He continued the withdrawal of British forces and would have been prepared to recognize Miguel in return for certain guarantees.

Palmerston on the contrary chose to identify himself very closely with Maria's party. He may have been influenced in this by the letters and despatches of Frederick Lamb, the brother of Lord Melbourne and Lady Cowper, who had recently arrived in Lisbon as the British Minister. Lamb became very partisan and wrote critical, even rude, letters to Lord Dudley, when he was still Foreign Secretary, because he thought that Dudley was luke-warm about the matter.[7]

In his speech of 1 June 1829 Palmerston threw down the gauntlet to the Wellington government on Portugal as well as on Greece. He began with a comprehensive denunciation of Miguel – 'this destroyer of constitutional freedom, this breaker of solemn oaths, this faithless usurper, this enslaver of his country, this trampler upon public law, this violator of private rights, this attempter of the life of helpless and defenceless woman.' English honour, he maintained, was involved in the support of Maria. Miguel, who had returned to Portugal with British blessing, had betrayed them. 'Was it fitting', he demanded 'that the King of England should be made the stalking-horse, under whose cover this royal poacher should creep upon his unsuspecting prey?' Palmerston was beginning to show unexpected eloquence. Southgate sees this speech as a deliberate bid for the Foreign Office.[8] This is doubtful in the political circumstances of the time but Palmerston was certainly presenting to the world his interpretation of Canningite foreign policy.

Palmerston may have seen himself as Canning's legatee but in fact he had considerably changed the approach. Canning had been happy to sway Parliament and the public by eloquent, if sometimes rather vague, appeals to nationalism and constitutionalism. He was the master of the memorable phrase, but his policy had been essentially cautious. 'Let us not', he told the Commons in March 1821 'in the foolish spirit of romance, suppose that we alone could regenerate Europe . . . The price at which political liberty is to be valued and the cost at which it is to be obtained, constitute the nicest balance and one which only those immediately interested in the calculation are competent to decide.'[9]

Palmerston's speech of June 1829 struck a very different note. Peel had already spoken and defended what had become the classical doctrine of non-intervention, as defined by Lord Castlereagh, namely that every nation had the right to manage its own internal affairs as it pleased, so long as it did not injure its neighbours. Palmerston told the House, 'Time was, and that but lately, when England was regarded by all Europe, as the friend of liberty and civilization, and therefore of happiness and prosperity, in every land; because it was thought that her rulers had the wisdom to discover, that the selfish interests and political influence of England, were best promoted, by the extension of liberty and civilization. Now, on the contrary, the prevailing opinion is, that England thinks her advantage to lie, in withholding from other countries that constitutional liberty, which she herself enjoys.'

So far as non-intervention was concerned, Palmerston agreed that other nations had no right to intervene 'by force of arms' but he pleaded for a right to 'interfere' in every way 'short of actual force'. Where the distinction lay was not made clear in the rest of the speech, where he again seemed to be thinking of forcible intervention. He had no difficulty in establishing that Canning had repeatedly 'interfered' in Portugal up to 1827. He felt this to be justified, partly by ancient treaties, but more by strategic considerations. 'It has been thought', he said, 'by the most competent judges, that with Gibraltar our own, and with an ally at Lisbon, we might face the combined hostility of France and Spain . . . without alarm.'[10]

There is no evidence that the speech made any great impact at the time, although it attracted some attention as a deliberate copy of Canning's style. Palmerston was not regarded as a foreign affairs expert. He did not have the first-hand knowledge that Wellington had of Portugal or Aberdeen of Greece. The House of Commons was half empty and the version in Hansard is one which Palmerston himself supplied later and so may not be exactly what he said. But Palmerston also circulated copies to the press and obviously himself regarded it as a very important statement.

On the other hand, Wellington does not seem to have taken it too seriously as an attack on his policy; at least, he made several attempts to bring Palmerston back into his ministry, although not it is true in any office connected with foreign affairs. However liberal a stance Palmerston was taking on foreign questions, he still seemed safely conservative on most domestic questions. He had admittedly supported Catholic Emancipation in 1829 and even made two powerful parliamentary speeches on the subject but he had never made any secret of his view that the only alternative was a civil war in Ireland and always placed his support on the most conservative possible grounds. He was much more cautious on parliamentary reform. Reform proposals took two rather different forms. Some wanted a measure of redistribution to give the new manufacturing towns their own representation and this commanded the support of some quite conservative men. Others also wanted an extension of the franchise and this was considered much more risky. Palmerston had little difficulty in accepting the first, but he was doubtful about the second.[11] Nevertheless, it was parliamentary reform which took Palmerston, together with the other Canningites, from the Tory to the Whig side of the House.

In July 1830 a revolution in France overthrew the increasingly autocratic Charles X in favour of the representative of the younger branch of the Bourbon family, the Duke of Orleans, who assumed the title of King Louis Philippe and undertook to govern in a strictly constitutional manner. A month earlier George IV had died, necessitating a general election in Britain. At first Wellington thought that the troubles in France would make the property owning class in Britain rally strongly to the Tory side. In fact, the new House of Commons, which met in the autumn of 1830 was, in the language of the day, very 'loose' with party allegiances confused and ill-defined. Wellington's uncompromising stand against any parliamentary reform cost him vital support and he resigned on 16 November.

Wellington had been aware for some time that his government team in the Commons required reinforcement. The Canningites, led by Palmerston after Huskisson's dramatic death under the wheels of Stephenson's *Rocket* in September 1830, were small in numbers but included men of experience and talent. Both Whigs and Tories angled for their support. The final break between Palmerston and Wellington came very late. On 6 November the Tory, J.W. Croker, called to urge Palmerston to reconsider Wellington's offer of a place in his Cabinet but, when Palmerston remained unpersuaded, he asked him the blunt question, 'Are you resolved, or are you not, to vote for Parliamentary Reform?' When Palmerston said he was, Croker replied, 'Well, then, there is no use talking to you any more on this subject. You and I, I am grieved to see, shall never sit on the same bench again.'[12]

Palmerston had indeed made his final break with the Tory party with which he had been associated since 1806. When the veteran Whig, Lord Grey, formed his administration towards the end of November 1830 he asked Palmerston to join it. It was not at first intended that Palmerston should go to the Foreign Office. Grey had hoped to keep that office in his own hands and, when that proved impracticable, he thought first of Lord Lansdowne or Lord Holland for the job. It was initially proposed that Palmerston should become Leader of the House of Commons and Chancellor of the Exchequer but the Leadership was subsequently offered to Althorpe and Palmerston was proposed instead for the Home Office. Madam Lieven flattered herself that she suggested to Grey that Palmerston should have the Foreign Office. She greatly exaggerated her political influence — even though she was Grey's mistress at the time — but she did approve of the arrangement, providing further proof that many people did not take Palmerston's new liberal stance and denunciation of the Holy Alliance Powers too seriously.

Palmerston did not play a prominent part in the domestic controversies of the next few years, notably the stormy passage of the Great Reform Act of 1832. He still had many reservations about parliamentary reform. He had spoken in favour of what was sometimes called 'piecemeal' reform in both 1829 and 1830, mainly on the good Whig grounds that timely reform staved off revolution and that the remedying of certain obvious abuses would make more far-reaching changes unnecessary, but he became increasingly uneasy as the Great Reform Bill took shape. Charles Greville's note in his *Memoirs* that Lady Cowper told him that Palmerston detested and abhorred 'the whole thing' is probably exaggerated but Palmerston certainly had contacts with the group known as the 'Waverers', led by Lord Harrowby, who tried for a compromise measure. In particular, he disliked the proposal to flood the House of Lords with new peers if they continued to reject the Bill as passed by the Commons. He poured out his objections to Grey in a letter on 8 April 1831 to which Grey replied that Palmerston's letter had given him 'some pain' but that he, Grey, was committed beyond the possibility of retreat. He suggested that they talk the matter over.[13]

Grey's handling of Palmerston in these years was superbly tactful and the latter never seems to have seriously contemplated resignation. In retrospect, the Great Reform Act seems an extremely modest measure. When Palmerston looked round the House of Commons elected in 1833, the first under the new dispensation, he commented with relief that it did not look very different from its predecessors. Parliamentary reform had, however, cost Palmerston the Cambridge University seat, to which he was so attached. He had in fact been defeated at the general election of May 1831 − concern about the attitude of his Cambridge constituents had probably done something to influence his attitude in the spring of 1831 − and he was temporarily accommodated at the burgage borough of Bletchingley in Surrey, which was ironically scheduled for abolition under the Bill. In 1833 he fought and won the large county constituency of South Hampshire but he lost it in 1835. Desperate for a seat, he paid the Whig MP for Tiverton in Devon, James Kennedy, £2,000 to resign − he also helped Kennedy's family with some Foreign Office patronage. Palmerston was returned unopposed at the ensuing by-election and retained the Tiverton constituency for the rest of his life.

5

Foreign Secretary under Grey and Melbourne

In 1829–30 Palmerston had proclaimed Canningite doctrine as he saw it in the field of foreign affairs. His motives for doing so were at least partly rooted in domestic politics. In the confused politics of those years it was important that the Canningites should maintain a clear identity. Canning had become so associated with the conduct of foreign policy that it was easier to raise the standard in that field, while foreign questions were less divisive among potential supporters than were some domestic questions. In so doing Palmerston had given a distinctly ideological slant to the debate. Britain stood for the upholding of constitutional rights in other countries and for the extension of liberty and civilization. There is no real evidence that Palmerston sought the Foreign Office in preference to any other office in 1830 but it was to the Foreign Office that he went and it is therefore possible to test his actions against his words.

One question must, however, be asked first. How far was Palmerston's policy his own, at least in the early days of the Whig ministry up to the summer of 1834, while Lord Grey remained Prime Minister? Contemporaries tended to see the policy, particularly in its generally (not invariably) pro-French slant, as being that of Grey, and the great battles on foreign affairs taking place in the Lords between Grey and Wellington. Professor Webster in his massive study of Palmerston's policy up to 1841 was conviced that, although Palmerston was only able to triumph over his many opponents in the Cabinet because of Grey's support, 'the initiative and the conduct of policy remained in Palmerston's hands throughout'.[1] This is difficult to sustain in the light of the evidence of the Broadlands Papers where Grey's correspondence with Palmerston, especially at the beginning, shows Grey guiding Palmerston very carefully, although very tactfully, on almost every decision of importance. Bourne, in his more recent work, shifts the emphasis and sees a kind of inner Cabinet emerging on foreign affairs, consisting of Grey, Palmerston, Lansdowne and Holland. In his early years at the Foreign Office, Palmerston certainly did not have the free hand and the prestige that he enjoyed later. Under Melbourne from 1835 to 1841, he had more independence but he was still often engaged in a difficult balancing act, trying to conciliate or neutralize opinions hostile to his own.

When Palmerston went to the Foreign Office in November 1830, the outstanding questions were connected with the recent revolution in France. Palmerston himself had visited Paris twice in 1829 and had shown more foresight than many, including the British Ambassador, Lord Stuart de Rothesay, in anticipating an immediate smash if Charles X persisted with his policies. When the revolution came in July 1830, Palmerston greeted it with delight. He wrote to his brother-in-law, Henry Sulivan, 'We shall drink the cause of Liberalism all over the world. Let Spain and Austria look to themselves; this reaction cannot end where it began & Spain & Italy & Portugal & parts of Germany will sooner or later be affected. This event is decisive of the ascendancy of Liberal Principles throughout Europe; the evil spirit has been put down and will be trodden underfoot. The reign of Metternich is over . . .'[2] To his Canningite colleague, Charles Grant, he wrote, 'Well what a glorious event this is in France! How admirably the French have done it! What energy and courage in the day of trial: and what wisdom and moderation in the hour of victory'! He contrasted the restraint of 1830 with the excesses of 1792–3 and concluded that the change had been wrought by 'nothing but a short and imperfect enjoyment of a free Press and a free constitution'. He did not believe that the French would embark on an aggressive foreign policy as they had done under the First Revolution. 'From all I saw when I was at Paris my conviction is that the French will be quiet at home and abroad.'[3]

Palmerston had anticipated that Wellington would have to change his ultra-conservative foreign policy. Rather ironically, Wellington and Aberdeen, although they expressed themselves very differently, read events in France much as Palmerston had done. They saw it as a limited political revolution which Charles X had brought on himself and they did not believe that the government of Louis Philippe meant to be aggressive. The best way of preserving the peace of Europe was therefore to recognize the *fait accompli.*

More testing was the likelihood that, as Palmerston had recognized, the movement would not end in France. It spread first to Belgium, where disorders began in Brussels in August. In 1815 Belgium had been united with Holland under the Dutch King, William I. The union was not so grotesque as the liberals later contended. The two countries' economies were potentially complementary and the undeniable religious and linguistic divisions did not coincide with the frontier between Holland and Belgium; but some Belgians had resented the arrangement from the beginning. No one doubted that the Allies' real motive had been to provide a strong barrier to French expansion into the Low Countries.

That, of course, created the problem for a liberally-minded British Foreign Secretary. It was one thing for Palmerston out of office to rejoice in the spread of liberal principles and the trampling underfoot of Metternichism. It was quite another to acquiesce in an arrangement which might leave France free to move into Antwerp. There was also the danger that the Eastern Powers might decide to intervene whatever Britain did. Here too Wellington's government had acted pragmatically. They had established an ambassadorial conference in London and had accepted that the Belgians would not return to the arrangements of 1815, although they still hoped that they would agree to some kind of autonomy under William I. Palmerston was more convinced that the Belgians would settle for nothing less than full independence, although like Wellington he at first hoped that the Belgians would choose a prince of the House of Nassau as their ruler. In other ways too he found himself carrying on the policy of Wellington's government, which he had recently so comprehensively denounced. The London ambassadorial conference became his chief instrument of policy.

He used it with considerable skill as foreign diplomats, including the formidable Talleyrand, conceded. He was to some extent helped by circumstances. The outbreak of revolution in Poland distracted the Eastern Powers from Belgium. The government of Louis Philippe was too insecure to risk a serious quarrel with Britain. Nevertheless, Palmerston seems to have realized that he could apply some of the tactics he had learnt in the long years of in-fighting at the War Office to international diplomacy. He had had plenty of experience of mastering 'masses of detail and drafting endless papers' and it was for this, as Bourne says, 'in a mixture of contempt and admiration, he gained his first nickname in the Foreign Office of "Protocol Palmerston"'.[4] He also learnt in his early years at the Foreign Office that bluff often pays off. 'Lord Pumicestone', too, was emerging.

The Belgians drew up a new constitution for themselves and, in February 1831, elected the Duke of Nemours, the son of Louis Philippe, as their king. Louis Philippe, however, knowing that such a choice would be intolerable to the other Powers, vetoed it. Instead Leopold of Saxe-Coburg became Leopold I of the Belgians. William I, although he had reluctantly accepted the independence of Belgium in January 1831, was still spoiling for a fight and he found an excellent pretext in the renewed Belgian claim to the Grand Duchy of Luxembourg. In August 1831 a Dutch army entered Belgium and reached Brussels.

The crisis presented Palmerston with his first big challenge both at home and abroad. Leopold appealed for British and French help. A British fleet was sent to patrol the Channel but it was a French army which compelled the Dutch to withdraw. The Tory opposition in England immediately launched a strong attack on Palmerston's policy. The battle of Waterloo had been undone, they claimed. Palmerston's ineptitude had allowed the French to occupy Belgium. Palmerston put the blame on William I for acting without notifying the London Conference but this explanation further entangled him. The Dutch chargé in London had in fact delivered a note announcing the intended Dutch action on 3 August but, because it was addressed to Palmerston in his capacity as chairman of the Conference, he had not, he said, opened it until the Conference met the following day. His critics were not slow to suggest that it was Palmerston's notorious tendency to neglect public business for private pleasures, rather than a too strict adherence to protocol, which had caused the embarrassing delay. Palmerston had a rough passage in the Commons.[5]

In the Conference he did rather better. The Powers had agreed as early as January 1831 that Belgium should become an independent state and that the Powers should guarantee its neutrality. As the result of the events in the Low Countries the details of the agreement had to be modified in June and again in October 1831. The October terms, the Twenty-Four Articles, were ratified by the Powers in January 1832. The terms were acceptable to the Belgians but not to the Dutch. William I, who was still in control of Antwerp, refused to withdraw.

Palmerston was well aware that, although the French would have liked to have settled Belgium themselves, they dared not face war with Britain probably supported by the rest of Europe. He had leaned upon Louis Philippe to reject the Nemours' candidature and to accept Leopold. He leaned upon him even more strongly to withdraw the French forces in 1831. The technique he employed was typical of the period. He could have warned the French officially that certain actions would compel Britain to go to war. Instead he wrote privately to the British Ambassador in Paris, Lord Granville. His warnings culminated in the sharp letter of 17 August 1831, in which he wrote, 'One thing is certain — the French must go out of Belgium, or we have a general war, and war in a given number of days'. The letters were sent by post, not by diplomatic messenger. Palmerston was well aware that the French would 'intercept' and read the letters. The French, of course, were equally well aware that Palmerston knew and intended that. The warning was taken. The French troops were withdrawn.[6]

This, however, left the way open for William's new intransigence in 1832. Palmerston had already discovered what could be achieved by discreet threats of war, especially in an area which could be reached by British sea power. He now tried another technique, which was to become a favourite with him, that of allying with a potential enemy in order to restrict his freedom of action. In Palmerston's eyes in 1832 it was the Dutch King who was obstructing the settlement so tortuously reached by the Great Powers. He was, therefore, prepared to see a limited French military intervention aimed at getting the Dutch out of Antwerp so long as it was backed up by an Anglo-French blockade of the Scheldt and the Dutch port of Rotterdam. Palmerston had great difficulty in persuading both the King and Parliament of the desirability of this policy which seemed the complete reversal of the 'containment' of France intended in 1815. Nevertheless, Palmerston was correct in thinking that this would quickly compel the Dutch to withdraw and leave the French with no further excuse for intervention.

William withdrew his forces but still refused to sign a treaty with the Belgians who were thus left in *de facto* occupation of all they held at that moment, including part of Luxembourg. The London Conference remained in being until 1839 when a final settlement was reached. Although the Belgians gained better financial terms in 1839 than they had been offered in 1832, they were compelled to surrender some areas they had held since 1831. By 1839 Palmerston was on bad terms with France and anxious to align his policy more closely with that of the Eastern powers. But, like Canning, he had not really wished to crusade for a new Europe or even for Belgian self-determination. The guiding principle was the preservation of British interests, which in this case meant that France must not dominate the Low Countries.

Belgium was not the only country where revolution had erupted in 1830. Poland, Germany and Italy had all become involved. In Poland Palmerston could do no more than claim that, as a signatory of the Treaty of Vienna, Britain had the right to be consulted before Poland's status was changed. The Russians were not prepared to listen. By 1832 the Poles had lost their position as a quasi-autonomous constitutional monarchy under the Tsar of Russia, which they had gained in 1815, and become for all practical purposes another Russian province, under a harshly authoritarian regime.

In a number of the smaller German states the Liberals won new constitutions, but in Prussia and Austria the monarchies emerged unscathed. By 1832 the conservative *status quo* had, generally speaking, been restored. Palmerston showed no particular interest in Germany at this time. When Henry Bulwer, then an MP, later his biographer, challenged him to protest to Austria and Prussia that they were contravening the Treaty of Vienna, which guaranteed the independence of the German states, by coercing them into anti-revolutionary activities, Palmerston declined. In his opinion, he said, the Treaty had not been breached. He skilfully covered up his lack of action by a proclamation of his approval of constitutional states. 'Constitutional States', he declared in a famous passage, 'I consider to be the natural Allies of this country; and whoever may be in office conducting the affairs of Great Britain, I am persuaded that no English Ministry will perform its duty if it be inattentive to the interests of such States.'[7]

Italian struggles did command more of his sympathy but it is difficult to contend that he was able to achieve any more there than in Poland or Germany. There had been a number of unsuccessful risings in Italy in the 1820s and 1831–2 saw a number of outbreaks in central Italy, the most serious in Bologna, where the rebels proclaimed the abolition of the temporal power of the Papacy. The Pope's difficulties were a cause for rejoicing in England, where religious feelings still ran high. But, from the point of view of the Foreign Office, the important thing was to prevent a clash between Austria and France. The recently elected Pope, Gregory XVI, a strong conservative, appealed for Austrian help and the Austrians sent a force to Bologna. The French countered by sending a force to Ancona.

Palmerston was mainly anxious that the trouble in Italy should subside without further complications but he was also imbued with the Whig belief that reform staved off revolution. He therefore sent an unofficial emissary, Sir Brook Taylor, to the Pope. (Protestant England had no diplomatic relations with the Papacy). He told Taylor that he favoured an arrangement by which 'on the one hand the people of the Romagna should return to their obedience to the temporal authority of the Pope, and that on the other, the Pope should grant to his subjects such improvements in their Institutions and in the Form and administration of their government, as may remove the main part of those practical grievances which they have hitherto suffered'.[8] He did not venture to urge the establishment of representative government but he did suggest improvements in the judicial system, including the abolition of the Inquisition. The Pope took no notice. Absolutism was re-established throughout Italy and both the Austrian and the French troops were eventually withdrawn. War had been averted but the cause of liberalism had not been furthered.

The Iberian peninsula seemed a more promising field, in which Britain could assert herself. As in the Low Countries, Britain had acknowledged strategic interests. Canning had already involved her deeply in the affairs of Portugal. In the 1830s both Spain and Portugal suffered prolonged civil wars. In both it was possible to represent the struggle as one between absolutism and constitutionalism. The British public liked to think in these nice clear-cut terms and so Palmerston presented it to them. Those who had alternative sources of information were sceptical. It was not so much that they doubted that the supporters of Miguel in Portugal or of Carlos in Spain were absolutists as that they were unconvinced of the liberalism of their protagonists, Maria in Portugal and Isabella in Spain. They saw both struggles as essentially the disputes of internal factions and believed that Britain should have followed Castlereagh's strict doctrine of non-intervention.

When Palmerston went to the Foreign Office in November 1830, Miguel was in control of the whole of Portugal. Maria's supporters held only Terciera in the Azores; but, in April 1831, Pedro was compelled to abdicate from the throne of Brazil and determined to re-assert his daughter's claims to the Portuguese crown. He landed at Oporto in July 1832 but attracted little support. Palmerston turned a blind eye to the breaches of the Foreign Enlistment Act and allowed British sailors, notably Charles (later Admiral) Napier, to volunteer to serve under Pedro. Napier defeated Miguel's fleet off Cape St Vincent early in July 1833 and took possession of Lisbon three weeks later.

In Spain, too, the struggle centred on the rival claims of an uncle and a niece to the throne. In the 1820s the acknowledged heir of the king, Ferdinand VII, was his younger brother, Carlos, but in 1829 the widowed Ferdinand married Maria Christina of Naples. Carlos's supporters resented the marriage and dubbed Christina a 'Liberal', meaning it as a term of abuse. Christina gave birth to two daughters, Isabella and Louisa Fernanda. There was no traditional bar on women succeeding to the Spanish throne but some held that the Treaty of Utrecht of 1713 excluded them from the succession for fear of a union of the Spanish and French crowns. When Ferdinand died in September 1833, the Carlists resisted the accession of Isabella and the Regency of her mother, Christina. Carlos, like Miguel in Portugal, was supported by the clerical party. He also had the support of the separatists of Navarre and the Basque country. What was much more disturbing in Palmerston's eyes was the fact that he had the support of the three Eastern Powers, Russia, Prussia and Austria, who had very recently come together in the Münchengrätz agreement by which they pledged themselves to uphold the absolutist cause.

Palmerston determined on a counter-stroke. The government of Louis Philippe was well disposed to the Christinos, as the party of Isabella and her mother was known. If Britain and France were united, it would be impossible for the Eastern Powers to intervene. In April 1834 Palmerston secured the Quadruple Alliance of Britain, France and the governments of Christina and Maria. He was always immensely proud of it. 'A capital hit and all my own doing', he called it. He congratulated himself, 'It establishes a quadruple alliance among the constitutional states of the West, which will serve as a powerful counterpoise to the Holy Alliance of the East.'[9]

This was a new concept of the balance of power. The balance of power was a guiding principle which Palmerston proclaimed all through his long official life as Foreign Secretary or Prime Minister, but it was an ambiguous term. In the years after the Congress of Vienna of 1814–15, it was normally taken to mean the territorial balance established by the Vienna Settlement and designed to ensure that no Great Power became too great at the expense of its neighbours. The Quadruple Alliance represented in a very embryonic form the idea of two balancing power blocs, the absolutist Powers of the east and the constitutional Powers of the west.

Whether it was wise to divide Europe in this way, whether it really made for peace, was open to question. Palmerston himself seems to have regarded it as second best. He would have preferred to keep the old Concert of Europe alive – that is the system by which all the major Powers would meet round the conference table to settle difficult and dangerous questions. It had worked over both the Greek and the Belgian questions. Both those conferences had met in London. Palmerston would have been very happy indeed in the 1830s to see London become the diplomatic capital of Europe. The problem was that Metternich was equally convinced that Vienna was the natural centre for such activities. Between them, the ball slipped from their hands and, although the concept of a Concert of Europe never died in the nineteenth century, it never grew very substantial either.[10]

The Quadruple Alliance itself was always a very flimsy structure. Britain and France were uneasy allies and the other two partners, the governments of Maria and Christina, were hardly in control of their countries. The problems of Portugal were settled first. Miguel was not a good general, nor perhaps essentially a fighter. He never recovered from the reverses of the summer of 1833 and when he was defeated in May 1834, he agreed to surrender his claims to the throne and go into exile. The constitution of 1826 was restored and Palmerston's policy seemed triumphant.

Carlos was made of sterner stuff. Louis Philippe would have liked to send a French army to help Christina, not least because it would have improved his standing with the French people. But Palmerston was not prepared to countenance either the despatch of French troops or the intervention of a joint Anglo-French force. He would agree only to the sending of an Anglo-French naval squadron to patrol the coasts, although he was prepared to send money to Christina and to allow British volunteers to go to her aid. At first it seemed sufficient. In May 1834 Carlos surrendered to a British naval officer and was brought to England. Unfortunately for the British Foreign Office, the next act turned into farce. Carlos's forces continued to fight for him and the following year Carlos himself slipped quietly out of England and rejoined his army in the north of Spain. Christina was unpopular in many quarters and her supporters were split between the Moderados who wanted to see a strong monarchy and the Progressistas, led by General Espartero, who wanted to make the ministry dependent on the Cortes. For several years the struggle between the Carlists and the Christinos was very equally balanced. Only in the autumn of 1839 was Carlos decisively defeated by Espartero and again forced into exile. Palmerston's influence on the outcome in Spain had been much less than in Portugal but, in both countries, he had achieved what was probably his primary aim — that of preventing unilateral action by France.

Britain and France were not able to achieve the same degree of co-operation on the Eastern Question, which was about to enter a new and critical phase. The basic questions were still; could the Ottoman empire survive and, if not, what would take its place? Palmerston's first preferred solution, before he became Foreign Secretary, was as robust as his reactions to the Greek and Portuguese problems. Like Gladstone later he rather hoped that the Turks would leave Europe, bag and baggage. In September 1829, shortly before the treaty of Adrianople, when Russia seemed to have Turkey at her mercy, Palmerston wrote to his friend, Edward Littleton, expressing his regret that Russia was going to stop short of pressing her advantage to the point where the Ottoman empire would collapse. It was apparently Madame Lieven who had tipped Palmerston off that the Russians would not go to extremes because they believed that a weak Turkey would be a good neighbour and certainly preferable to the international complications of a partition. Palmerston wrote, 'I should not be sorry some day or other to see the Turk kicked out of Europe, & compelled to go and sit cross-legged, smoke his pipe, chew his opium, & cut off heads on the Asiatic side of the Bosphorous; we want civilization, activity, trade & business in Europe, & your Mustaphas have no idea of any traffic beyond rhubarb, figs & red slippers . . .' This was so inconsistent with Palmerston's later policy of bolstering up the Ottoman empire at all costs that, at a house party at Woburn Abbey in December 1856, Littleton suggested to Palmerston that he might like to alter the word 'sorry' to 'surprised', which he did, and it was in this form that the letter was subsequently published.[11]

Even in the 1830s Palmerston had begun to commit himself to the policy of bolstering up the Ottoman empire, although this time the threat to the Sultan came, not from Russia, but from the rebellious Pasha (Governor) of Egypt, Mehemet Ali, whom Palmerston deeply distrusted as a French protegé. Mehemet Ali, who had a great admiration for the emperor, Napoleon I, had been busy modernizing Egypt (with considerable success) with the help of French advisers. He had a good army and in 1824 the Sultan, Mahmud II, called on him for assistance in putting down the Greek rebels. In return, he promised him Crete and Syria. Mehemet Ali sent his adopted son, Ibrahim, to the Morea and, but for the intervention of the European Powers, Ibrahim would probably have crushed the Greek revolt completely. After the Greek settlement, Mehemet Ali demanded his promised reward but, in view of his limited success, Mahmud refused to grant him Syria, as well as Crete. Mehemet Ali determined to take Syria by force. Some believed that he meant to go further and make himself Sultan in Mahmud's place. In 1831 Ibrahim invaded and conquered Syria and Palestine. In December 1832 he defeated the Turkish army at Konieh and began to advance on the Bosporus.

The Sultan appealed to Britain for assistance. Palmerston would have been prepared to give it but he could not persuade the rest of the Cabinet. They had barely emerged from the Reform Bill crisis and were indeed in the middle of a general election. In any case they did not care for open-ended, and probably expensive, commitments where British interests were not obvious. Palmerston later wrote to Frederick Lamb, 'There is nothing that has happened since I have been in this office which I regret so much as that tremendous blunder of the English government. But it was not my fault; I tried hard to persuade the Cabinet to let me take the step. But Althorpe and Brougham and others, some from ignorance of the bearing of foreign affairs, some for one foolish reason, some for another, would not agree. Grey, who was with me on the point, was weak and gave way, and so nothing was done in a crisis of the utmost importance to all Europe, when we might with the greatest of ease have accomplished a good result.'[12]

In despair the Sultan turned to Russia. The result was the Treaty of Unkiar Skelessi of July 1833. It was an agreement that roused deep suspicions in the West although it was essentially a defensive agreement. There were, as the other Powers suspected, secret clauses, of which the most important was a Turkish undertaking to close the Dardanelles to all foreign warships if the Russians requested it.

An uneasy peace prevailed in the Near East until 1839. Syria was still under Ibrahim's control and Mahmud had been building up his army to expel him. By 1839 Mahmud had realized that he was a dying man and must act soon if he was to act at all. Ibrahim had little difficulty in defeating him and once again the way to Constantinople lay open. On 1 July Mahmud died and was succeeded by Abdul Mejid, a boy of sixteen. The dissolution of the Ottoman empire seemed imminent and all the Great Powers were seriously alarmed.

At this time Palmerston was more suspicious of France than of Russia in the Mediterranean. In 1830 Charles X had intervened in Algeria and the July Monarchy had, despite occasional apologies to Britain, steadily consolidated the French position there. The links between Mehemet Ali and France were strong and Palmerston was consequently very suspicious when the French urged the Sultan to grant further concessions to Mehemet Ali. Nevertheless he did make some attempts to co-ordinate his policy with that of France, just as he had over Belgium, but in the course of 1839 he moved closer to Russia and the break-down of relations between France and Britain really came when Thiers became Prime Minister of France in March 1840. Thiers was a man who in many ways resembled Palmerston himself. Palmerston was well aware that Thiers would have liked a success in foreign policy to establish himself with his own public, and he suspected that he was prolonging negotiations to allow time for a *fait accompli* to emerge in the Near East.

Palmerston threw in his lot with the three Eastern powers and signed a treaty with them, officially entitled a Convention for the Pacification of the Levant, on 15 July 1840. They agreed to offer Mehemet Ali Egypt 'for his house', that is to say the Governorship of Egypt was to become hereditary in his family, (previously Mehemet Ali had been an official, technically removable at the Sultan's will), and Syria for his lifetime. Mehemet Ali was given only twenty days in which to accept these terms. If he refused, it was made clear that the Great Powers would assist the Sultan in defeating him. Mehemet Ali proved obstinate and on 3 November 1840 a British fleet bombarded Acre. Mehemet Ali finally submitted on 8 December.

During the bombardment of Acre the British Admiral, Stopford, had had some fears that the French might intervene on the Egyptian side. The French were extremely indignant and began to speak in warlike terms. Just before the bombardment, Thiers had been replaced by Guizot, who had been recalled from being the French ambassador in London to head the ministry. Guizot himself was rightly regarded as both a pacific man and an Anglophile. Nevertheless, it was a close-run thing, with the French Cabinet divided into war and peace parties. In the end the matter was settled peacefully by a new treaty, to which France was a party, the Straits Convention of 13 July 1841, which related to the Dardanelles and the Bosporus. This forbade the passage of foreign warships, with certain ceremonial exceptions, through the Straits while the Ottoman empire was at peace, thus abrogating any special advantages Russia might have gained by the Treaty of Unkiar Skelessi.

Palmerston himself regarded his Near Eastern policy as a triumph. He published an enormous Blue Book, commonly called the Levant Papers, to explain to parliament and the public how the crisis had developed. The Conservatives were very willing to back him: his troubles came from within his own party. The Whigs were traditionally pro-French and very suspicious of Russia, a feeling which had intensified because of events in Poland. Many Whigs had close contacts in France and some used them to counter Palmerston's policy. Ashley Cooper, later Lord Shaftesbury, believed that Edward (Bear) Ellice, who had always resented the fact that Palmerston, and not his own friend, Lord Durham, had got the Foreign Office in 1830 and frequently made difficulties for him, this time went so far as to urge Thiers to resist Palmerston, telling him how many people in England disapproved of Palmerston's policy. Lansdowne corresponded freely with the former French Prime Minister, the duc de Broglie. Holland and Clarendon kept Guizot, while he was still ambassador in London, well informed of the divisions within the British Cabinet. The press, primed by Charles Greville, the Clerk to the Privy Council, Henry Reeve, the journalist, and probably Lord Clarendon as well, were very critical. Ironically, in view of later events, Lord Aberdeen used his influence with *The Times* to call off the attacks. As a final *reductio ad absurdum,* that lunatic, but popular propagandist, David Urquhart, circulated the whole Cabinet with a memorandum accusing Palmerston of high treason for his secret dealings with Russia. In the summer and autumn of 1840 few people, except Palmerston himself, thought that war could be avoided.

The year 1840 would not have been a good moment for Britain to go to war with France. She was already at war with China, and war with the United States also seemed imminent. The Chinese war, which had begun in 1839, became known to history as the Opium War but that can be misleading. Wider issues were involved, principally the British determination to open up the China trade in general and to compel Peking to adopt normal western diplomatic conventions. Nevertheless, opium smuggling was the flashpoint. The authorities in southern China, unable to board the British ships which were bringing in the opium, placed the small British trading community at Canton, including the British consul, Charles Elliot, under a form of house arrest. Palmerston had little sympathy for the smugglers. The Chinese, he said, had a perfect right to ban the trade and punish those who engaged in it – although he did add the cynical comment that the Chinese grew opium themselves and that their objections to the foreign trade were probably on protectionist, rather than health, grounds. But the arrest of innocent British citizens and, more particularly, of a British consul was another matter. Palmerston's actions were to some extent pre-empted by the British government in India which had already sent assistance to Canton but Palmerston whole-heartedly backed them. William Gladstone might denounce him in the Commons and complain that the British flag was 'hoisted to protect an infamous contraband trade' but on this Palmerston generally had public support behind him.[13]

Britain had a number of outstanding disputes with America at this time but the two most serious turned on the slave trade and the Canadian boundary. Palmerston's hatred of the slave trade was deep and sincere, although he seems to have arrived at that conviction slowly. Both Britain and the United States had declared the trade illegal in 1807 and in 1815 the Congress of Vienna, under strong pressure from Lord Castlereagh, had also outlawed it. Enforcement, however, was another matter. In time of peace, a warship could only intercept a slaver flying her own colours. She had no jurisdiction over ships of other nations, no matter how blatant the offence. Since only the British kept a squadron on the West African coast at all regularly to check the trade, many slavers got through. After 1815, Britain negotiated treaties with many of the smaller nations of Europe, permitting British warships to arrest slavers flying their flags. Larger nations were harder to convince but in 1831 and 1833 Palmerston himself negotiated treaties of this type with France. In 1838 he seemed on the verge of one of his greatest triumphs in securing the adhesion of all the Great

Powers of Europe to one treaty, the Quintuple Treaty, which would have permitted a common 'Right of Search' over all slavers. It was French anger over Palmerston's conduct on the Eastern Question which led them to withhold ratification from the Quintuple Treaty and it never became effective as intended.

The United States had consistently refused to enter into any 'Right of Search' arrangements with Britain. Their intransigence sprang in part from their anger at the use Britain had made of 'Maritime Rights' over neutral ships during the Napoleonic Wars but mainly from the strong vested interests of the slave-owning Southern States. Palmerston conceded that British warships could not touch American slavers without a treaty agreement but he was angered by the fact that slavers of other nations, with whom Britain did have treaties, had begun to run up the Stars and Stripes on the approach of a British warship. He therefore argued for a more limited right, the 'Right of Visit' to check whether a suspected ship was entitled to the colours she was flying. Surely, he said, the Americans would not want slavers to escape simply by hoisting 'a piece of bunting'. It was a typical Palmerston phrase and it immediately inflamed feelings in America, where Palmerston was accused of having insulted the American Flag by calling it a mere 'piece of bunting'.[14]

Feeling was already running high because of the Canadian question. Basically, many Americans resented the fact that there was still a British colony on American soil at all, and the matter was kept open by the fact that the boundary line between the United States and British North America was still unsettled west of the Rocky Mountains and, more immediately dangerously, between Maine and New Brunswick. As settlers penetrated into these areas clashes of jurisdiction were inevitable. In 1837–8 there were two small-scale rebellions in Upper and Lower Canada (the modern Ontario and Quebec), provoked by local issues and easily suppressed, but some Americans, anxious to 'liberate' Canada, ran guns across the border. In the most dramatic incident of the affair, an American steamer, the *Caroline* was sunk in the Niagara river and an American, Amos Durfee, killed. Much later, in November 1840, a Canadian, Alexander McLeod, was arrested while doing business in New York state and charged with Durfee's murder. It is unlikely that McLeod had been concerned and, in any case, the British government immediately repeated what it had said at the time, that the sinking of the *Caroline* was an act of state for which individuals could not be held responsible. The Federal Government initially replied that they could not intervene in the judicial processes of the State of New York. Palmerston ordered the British

Minister in Washington, Henry Fox, to leave immediately if McLeod was executed. The Americans made the extraordinary reply that they would prevent him from doing so. In the end McLeod was acquitted but the matter still hung in the balance when Melbourne's government resigned in September 1841.

Palmerston was furious. He always hated losing office and, on his own estimation, his party was being swept from power on domestic questions in which he had never taken much interest, while his own policy in many fields was about to come to fruition. But popular and parliamentary sympathy was not on the whole with him at this time. The Tories, who had supported him over the Mehemet Ali question, were annoyed that Palmerston seemed to make no effort to improve relations with the French once the crisis was over, but rather to crow over them. There were those who would have agreed with Charles Greville when he wrote, 'Everything may possibly turn out according to his expectations. He is a man blessed with extraordinary good fortune, and his motto seems to be that of Danton, *De l'audace . . .* But there is flippancy in his tone, an undoubting self-sufficiency, and a levity in discussing interests of such tremendous magnitude, which satisfies me that he is a very dangerous man to be entrusted with the uncontrolled management of our foreign affairs.'[15] Those doubts were intensified among those whose opinions counted by his apparently factious opposition when he was out of office from 1841 to 1846.

6

Foreign Secretary under Russell

The years 1841–6 were a period of great frustration for Palmerston. Peel's administration restored normal relations with France and settled the outstanding differences with the United States. Palmerston accused his successor at the Foreign Office, Lord Aberdeen, of weakness. 'Our foreign affairs', he wrote to Lansdowne 'seem to have got upon a sliding scale, as well as the corn duties, and we are in that respect sliding downwards, by a very decently rapid descent.' He accused the government of sacrificing the 'permanent interests of the country in order to procure relief from momentary embarrassments'.[1] He suspected that Aberdeen was incapable of bluffing an opponent and, as he told Bulwer, every country would give up three out of four questions at issue rather than go to war but one should never let an opponent know which three.

He decided to launch a great attack on the Ashburton–Webster treaty which, on 1842, settled the most pressing disputes with America. The first skirmishes came in the press. The *Globe* was friendly to Palmerston and he sometimes wrote for it but his chief link at this time was with the *Morning Chronicle*. He had been introduced to its proprietor, John Easthope, in 1834. Easthope became a great admirer of Palmerston, who secured a baronetcy for him in 1841 and, more importantly, supplied him with inside information in return for consistent political support. When Parliament met in 1843 Palmerston transferred his campaign to the floor of the House and denounced the treaty. The result was a humiliating defeat. The House was 'counted out' for lack of a quorum. His tactics also caused renewed trouble with his party. Bedford, Spencer, Lord John Russell, Clarendon and Lansdowne joined together to warn him that they might feel compelled to repudiate publicly the line he was taking. Charles Greville noted, 'He ought to have felt the public pulse . . . It is now evident that he will not carry the public nor even his own party with him'.[2]

Greville was right. Palmerston's protests were echoed in some quarters but most people felt that the Conservative government was doing well in keeping foreign affairs peaceful while important reforms went forward at home. Distrust of Palmerston was still so strong even within his own party that, when Peel first resigned in December 1845 over the Corn Law crisis, Lord Grey (the son of Grey of the Reform Act) refused to join Lord John Russell's projected cabinet if Palmerston returned to the Foreign Office. Russell was unable to form a government and Peel resumed office for several months. Palmerston took the warning and, at Easter 1846, went to Paris, where he had a rather ostentatious reconciliation with the French Prime Minister, Guizot. The Court shared the misgivings of some of Palmerston's former colleagues and Palmerston wrote a long letter to Melbourne, intended to be shown to the Queen, protesting against the 'notion that I am more indifferent than I ought to be as to running the risk of war'. He insisted that his influence had always really been exerted on the side of peace and that the proof of that was that he had succeeded 'in preserving it unbroken during ten years of great and extraordinary difficulty'.[3]

When the Whig government came into office in July 1846 following Peel's resignation over the Corn Laws, Palmerston did return to the Foreign Office. There was an immediate deterioration in relations with France. One outstanding question was the marriage of the young queen of Spain, Isabella, and her sister, the Infanta Louisa Fernanda. The French had wanted the choice to be confined to princes of the House of Bourbon, mainly to exclude the possibility of Isabella marrying a Saxe-Coburg. (Queen Maria of Portugal was already married to a Coburg cousin of the Prince Consort). Aberdeen, although maintaining that the decision was entirely a matter for the Spaniards, was prepared to reach a 'gentleman's agreement' with Guizot that Isabella's choice should be restricted to the House of Bourbon, so long as Louis Philippe's sons were excluded from the list, and that the Infanta too, should not marry a son of Louis Philippe, at least until her sister was not only married but had children.

Palmerston was aware of the understanding when he returned to office. Nevertheless, he wrote a despatch to Bulwer, then the British Minister in Madrid, in which he named Leopold of Saxe-Coburg as a possible suitor for Isabella. This was the more provocative because Bulwer had recently been a party to an intrigue by Christina to reinstate Leopold as a candidate. Princess Lieven obtained a copy of the despatch and gave it to Guizot, whose mistress by this time she was, but it was an unnecessary piece of espionage. Palmerston did not regard the despatch as a breach of the Anglo–French understanding and showed a copy to the French *chargé* in London. But Guizot, who was probably glad of an excuse to break what was becoming a politically embarrassing agreement, declared that he resumed his freedom of action and arranged a double marriage of Isabella to a Spanish Bourbon, the Duke of Cadiz, and of the Infanta to the Duke of Montpensier, a younger son of Louis Philippe. The arrangement seemed particularly sinister in view of contemporary doubts as to whether Isabella's marriage would prove fertile. In fact Isabella did have children and, in 1870, was succeeded on the Spanish throne by her son, Alphonso XII, even though Isabella herself had been deposed in 1868.

In the long run the marriage had little effect on Franco-Spanish relations and Guizot tried to laugh it off as of no consequence, but that was not how it was taken in Britain. Some argued that the marriages were a breach of the Treaty of Utrecht of 1713. Legally, they were probably mistaken but the reaction in Britain from the Prince Consort downwards was an explosion of indignation at French 'treachery'. Arguably some of the blame was Palmerston's for clumsy handling of a delicate matter but, this time, all the anger was directed outwards towards France and some of it rebounded on Palmerston's predecessors, Aberdeen, and to a lesser extent, Peel, for being gullible in trusting the French.

Palmerston was equally adroit in evading blame for the difficult situation developing in Portugal. When the radical Septembrist party won the general election of 1845, Queen Maria, the darling of the English Liberals in the 1830s, dissolved the Cortes, annulled the constitution and conferred dictatorial powers on Marshal Saldanha. In October 1846 the Septembrists seized Oporto and Maria asked for assistance from Britain and France under the terms of the Quadruple Treaty of 1834. Palmerston, who had originally expressed some sympathy with the Septembrists, was acutely embarrassed but, in May 1847, he allowed the British navy to aid the Portuguese government in blockading Oporto. Maria was persuaded to restore constitutional government but this was largely a cosmetic operation; Saldanha and his right-wing supporters remained in power. Nevertheless, Palmerston's reputation for supporting constitutional causes remained intact.

Palmerston was now beginning to show some of the virtuosity in commanding public opinion which was to remain with him for the rest of his life. In the autumn of 1846 the Austrians annexed Cracow, all that remained of a free Poland. Poland had always been a popular cause in France and Guizot, under pressure from French liberals, suggested to

Palmerston that Britain and France should send a joint protest at this clear breach of the Vienna Settlement. Palmerston was not sorry to have a chance to snub Guizot and politely informed him that the British protest had already gone. Since Austria had secured the approval of Russia and Prussia for her action, an Anglo-French protest would have been little more than a gesture but the incident shows the breakdown of the embryonic western constitutional alignment of the 1830s. British public opinion, however, was satisfied by Palmerston's criticism of the Austrian action at the Lord Mayor's Banquet in November 1846.

Worsening relations with England were at one time supposed to have compelled Guizot to make his peace with Metternich and to allow French policy to become increasingly dependent on the Eastern powers. This dependence, it was argued, irritated the French people and contributed to the downfall of both Guizot and Louis Philippe in February 1848. Palmerston thus enjoyed a very sweet revenge for French treachery over the Spanish marriages.[4] The picture was not as simple as that. Britain and France continued to co-operate where they needed to, as in Portugal and in South America, where a long-running war between Argentina and Uruguay was disrupting trade on the River Plate. But Britain and France were unable to concert their policy in Switzerland.

In 1846 a simmering dispute between the seven Catholic cantons, the Sonderbund, and the twelve Protestant cantons boiled over. The quarrel was essentially about the powers of the Federal government, where the Protestant majority was pressing for liberal reforms, but it came to centre on the status of the Jesuit order. Previously, the Catholics had generally relied on Austrian support while the Protestants depended on liberal sympathy. In 1846, for various reasons, Charles Albert of Piedmont and Protestant Prussia were on the Austrian side, when Guizot too aligned his policy with that of Metternich. Surrounded by hostile powers, the Swiss government would have had little chance as the situation in Switzerland slipped towards civil war. They appealed to Britain. Protestant feeling in Britain was on their side but Palmerston was well aware that there was little he could do if the continental Powers were united against them. Throughout most of 1847 he played for time by suggesting an international conference — on the grounds that, since the Swiss constitution had been established by the Treaty of Vienna, any change in it was of international concern — and advised the radical government now in power in Switzerland not to attack the Sonderbund. They ignored this advice and attacked and captured the Catholic canton of Fribourg in November. The Sonderbund largely collapsed and it was too late in the year for the other

Powers to come to its assistance. Probably they would have intervened in 1848 but by then they had been overtaken by revolution themselves.

Palmerston's reputation had come to be very closely bound up with the fate of the Swiss Liberals. In the autumn of 1847 he had sent his old friend, Gilbert Elliot, now the second Earl of Minto, on a special mission to the Pope. On the way he called at the Swiss capital, Berne. While there, on Palmerston's instructions, he urged caution and delay but in retrospect it seemed very suspicious to European conservatives that his visit was immediately followed by the attack on Fribourg. Their suspicions seemed to be confirmed when a letter from Palmerston to the British Minister in Berne leaked. In it he suggested that an 'amicable arrangement' might be easier to arrive at if Fribourg were taken. In fact, the letter could have been no effect since it was written after the event.

Minto's whole mission came to have a sinister significance to European conservatives in the light of later events in Italy and elsewhere, although it could scarcely have been more innocent in origin. Palmerston had been encouraged by the apparent, and totally unexpected, liberality of the new pontiff, Pius IX, and Minto's mission had three very practical objectives. He was to try to persuade the Pope to use his influence to calm the situation in Ireland, which was still suffering from the dreadful consequences of the potato blight; to convince him that timely reforms in Italy were the best way to prevent revolutionary outbreaks, with all the attendant dangers of international complications; and to ask him to withdraw the Jesuits from Switzerland to give the situation there time to settle down. The last point was one reason why Minto counselled delay to the Swiss radicals in Berne but, just as he was suspected of triggering the Swiss civil war, so he was suspected of fermenting the insurrections which broke out in Italy in the early months of 1848.

The risings began on 12 January in Palermo. The Sicilians expelled the Neapolitan troops and an insurrection began in Naples itself. The following month the king, Ferdinand II, granted his people a constitution. Pius IX and the Duke of Tuscany also proclaimed constitutions. In the north, the Austrians held firm. The so-called 'Tobacco riots' in Lombardy, directed against heavy taxes on tobacco, only caused Metternich to substitute military control under the aged Marshall Radetzky for civilian government.

But the situation changed dramatically in the last week of February 1848. In France Guizot's government, with its narrow base of support among the upper bourgeoisie, had become more and more unpopular. A demonstration, aimed at compelling Louis Philippe to change his ministry, turned into a riot, and a riot into a revolution. On 24 February, Louis Philippe abdicated. A Provisional government, headed by the poet, Alphonse de Lamartine, was set up, a republic proclaimed, and elections, based on universal suffrage, called.

European governments began to fall like ninepins. On 13 March, riots broke out in Vienna. The following day Metternich fled, ignominiously hidden in a laundry basket. In April the Emperor, the near-imbecile Ferdinand, granted a constitution but further risings compelled him to abdicate in favour of his nephew, Francis Joseph. Separate insurrections, with nationalist aims, broke out in Bohemia, Hungary and northern Italy. The revolution in Berlin was directed at compelling the king, Frederick William IV, not only to grant a new constitution, but also to place himself at the head of a German nationalist movement, which would unite the whole country. In May 1848 an elected assembly met in Frankfurt to speak for the whole of Germany. Briefly Frederick William and the other princes seemed prepared to co-operate with this.

Only Russia and Britain appeared to stand outside the turmoil which was engulfing the whole of Europe, and Britain was by no means entirely exempt. In April 1848 the Chartists planned a monster demonstration on Kennington Common, from where they would march to the Houses of Parliament bringing their five-million signature petition demanding, among other things, universal suffrage. Some believed that they meant to set up a provisional government on the French model. Certainly, in Ireland some waited for a signal from London to start their own rising.

Palmerston reacted exactly like any other Englishman of property. He took command personally of the force of special constables assigned to the defence of the Foreign Office. No doubt he happily relived his days as a 'Volunteer' at Cambridge. He wrote to Lord Normanby, the British Ambassador in Paris, the next day, 'Yesterday was a glorious day, the Waterloo of peace and order. They say there were upwards of 100,000 special constables – some put the number at 250,000; but the streets were swarming with them, and men of all classes and ranks were blended together in defence of law and property.' It had been rumoured that the Chartists would be led by foreign agitators and Palmerston told Normanby, 'The foreigners did not show; but the constables, regular and special, had sworn to make an example of any whiskered and bearded rioter whom they might meet with, and I am convinced would have mashed them to jelly.'[5] The Chartist demonstration was smaller than expected and easily suppressed. There were, however, some outbreaks in Ireland, which were the more seriously regarded by the British government because there were known to have been contacts between the Irish leaders and some of the more left-wing leaders in Paris.

At first, Palmerston was implacable in his hostility to the Chartists. He had been a member of Melbourne's government at the time of the Newport rising in 1839 and had shared in the general alarm.[6] The Newport Chartists had been transported, as were the leaders of the Irish outbreaks. Occasional motions were introduced into the Commons for the pardon of first the Newport, and later the Irish, Chartists. Palmerston consistently voted against these but as Home Secretary he eventually agreed in 1854 that the Chartist and Irish leaders remaining in Van Diemen's Land should be freed on condition that they did not return to the United Kingdom. The condition was lifted two years later. Rather curiously, Palmerston had championed the cause of one Chartist, Mason, who in 1842 had been arrested and imprisoned for defying a ban on an open-air meeting, but he did this in the sacred name of freedom of speech.

Palmerston was clearly as frightened of revolution as was any other conservative in mid-nineteenth-century Britain. Nor did he sympathize very much with the economic distress which lay behind the outbreaks: at best he regarded this as something quite outside human control. Market forces and the iron laws of economics must be allowed to prevail. His own Irish estates had been badly affected by the famine but he wrote angrily to Russell in March 1847 that he could not be expected to do anything about it. The Sligo estate produced, he said, a gross rental of £4,000, out of which he had to meet many charges. On the estate there were about 6,000 persons 'whom some of our Friends would call *my* Poor, & say that I ought to employ & support' but they had grown to such numbers 'wholly without any consent, concurrence or Encouragement of mine'. Now that their accustomed food had 'vanished by a Dispensation of Providence', they were ten times more numerous than would be required for the profitable cultivation of the land and many times more numerous than the income from the land would enable him to employ. The only solution he could see was emigration but how could landlords finance that when their rents were not paid? He then put forward a practical suggestion – the government should advance money to the landlords to send out emigrants, just as it already did to finance drainage schemes.[7]

In fact, Palmerston did resort to the expedient of emigration. He seems to have taken little personal interest except to order that the emigrants be provided with rum punch on the ships – until the temperance societies objected and he changed the order to coffee and biscuits. Unhappily, he left the more important details to his agents, Kincaid and Stewart. The

Sligo emigrations became some of the most notorious of the 'landlord emigrations'. Angry Canadian authorities protested to the Colonial Office that the emigrants were all widows with helpless children and old men and women 'riddled with disease'. They had been sent out in conditions 'as bad as the slave trade', in dangerously overcrowded ships with insufficient food and hardly any clothing. Many died on the way. Those who survived had been promised a small sum of money on disembarkation in Quebec but no one had arrived to pay it and they had been abandoned to the Canadian winter. The complaints were sent to Palmerston but he only transmitted Kincaid and Stewart's reply to Lord Elgin, then the Governor General of Canada, without comment. The agents' reply amounted to saying that the emigrants had begged to go, that they were of the lowest class and that Palmerston would hardly have spent money sending them, if they had been any use as tenants at home.[8]

Palmerston's belief in the inevitability of economic forces and the unwisdom of restraining them would have rung more true, if he had applied them when his own interests were at stake. In fact, he had objected to the repeal of the Corn Laws in 1845. He wrote to Russell, complaining that Russell had sold the party to Richard Cobden. In the south, he said, they were not yet illuminated by this 'brilliant aurora Borealis'. He did not agree that corn should not be an exemption to free trade. They must have duties for revenue purposes. Otherwise there would have to be an increase in direct taxes 'amounting to a practical Confiscation of all Income arising from accumulated Capital'. As for the argument that duties should not be laid on 'the Food and Clothing of the mass of the People', they would then have to abolish the duties on tea, coffee, sugar and tobacco as well. He sneered at the possibility of Russell as Leader of the Commons in 'Lord Cobden's administration'.[9]

In all this Palmerston was, of course, being no more blind or self-interested than many other English and Irish landlords of the period. The amazing thing is that, at exactly the same time, he was gaining a reputation as an advanced liberal and radical, hated by the European conservatives who believed that he wished to overturn the whole social order.

The starting-point was undoubtedly Minto's mission to Italy. In line with Palmerston's belief that reform staved off revolution, Minto encouraged the king, Charles Albert of Piedmont-Sardinia, and the Duke of Tuscany, as well as the Pope himself, not to be deterred from necessary reforms by the fear of Austrian intervention. Sometimes he carried his enthusiasm rather far as when he appeared on a balcony at Genoa and cried *Viva l'Indipendenza Italiana*. In February 1848 he acted as mediator, at

Ferdinand's invitation, between Ferdinand and his Neapolitan subjects, although the mediation collapsed amid the general spread of European revolution.

There is no question of the sincerity of Palmerston's support for reform in Italy, which he regarded as hopelessly misgoverned, or his belief that the Austrians were largely responsible for the misgovernment. His sympathy for the cause of Italian unification was much more limited. Above all, he feared that the French would take advantage of the situation to re-establish their influence in Italy and, even more dangerously, place themselves at the head of the radical and revisionist forces in Europe. He played the diplomatic game with considerable skill during the next eighteen months.

The Austrians had been compelled to retreat from most of Lombardy by 22 March 1848. The same day, Manin declared a republic established in Venice. A few days later Charles Albert, against British and French advice, marched to help the Lombards. Ferdinand of Naples briefly declared his support for Charles Albert. The Sicilians, who had refused to return to their allegiance to Ferdinand, also threw in their lot with Charles Albert. The central duchies, Tuscany, Parma and Modena, too declared war on Austria. The tide began to turn when the Pope declared in April that he abhorred the idea of a war with Austria. Charles Albert was a hesitant leader. The deep fissures in the Italian nationalist movement began to show through and, on 25 July 1848, Radetzky decisively defeated Charles Albert at Custozza.

A compromise settlement still seemed possible. Britain and France had offered their mediation and Palmerston threatened the Austrians that, if they were obstinate, the British would not hold the French back from intervention. He made no bones about the fact that he would have liked the Austrians to have retreated north of the Alps which, he told Ponsonby, the British ambassador at Vienna, he believed Providence had set there to keep the Italians and the Germans apart since they were 'as unlike in everything as two races can be'.[10] But after Custozza he conceded that the Austrians would probably regain Venice. He still hoped that Lombardy and perhaps even some of the central duchies might join Piedmont. From the British point of view, this would have had the advantage of providing a strong barrier to France without involving Austria.

In November 1848 the Pope still further distanced himself from the revolution by fleeing from Rome to Gaeta. In February 1849 the Romans, led by Mazzini and Garibaldi, proclaimed the temporal power of the Pope abolished and a republic established. The following month Charles Albert renewed the war with Austria. Once again Radetzky defeated him, this time at Novara on 23 March. Charles Albert abdicated in favour of his son, Victor Emmanuel. The struggle for Italian independence was virtually over. The Pope appealed to the Powers to restore his territories. Louis Bonaparte, now in power in France and anxious for clerical support, responded. In June, French troops overthrew the Roman Republic. Two months later the Venetian Republic surrendered to the Austrians.

From Palmerston's point of view the struggle between Naples and Sicily provided the greatest embarrassment. In 1848 he had gone very far in his support of the Sicilian rebels. British warships had saluted (and so acknowledged) the Sicilian flag and he had even suggested that the Sicilians offer the crown to Charles Albert's son, the Duke of Genoa. They could not therefore, he told Russell in August 1848 'back out entirely' and 'leave Sicily to be a Prey to the Barbarites of a Neapolitan Invasion'. On the other hand, they were at peace with the King of Naples and the Treaty of Vienna acknowledged him as king of both kingdoms. The best Palmerston could suggest was that the British fleet, under Sir William Parker, maintained a watching brief and tried to dissuade the Neapolitans from crossing the Straits of Messina.[11] In this he was unsuccessful. Briefly in the winter of 1848–9 on their own initiative Parker and his French opposite number enforced an armistice on the two parties which Palmerston, very hesitantly, backed to allow time for negotiations. It encouraged the Sicilians to prolong their resistance but in the end left them to the vengeance of Ferdinand and the Neapolitans.

By the summer of 1849 the *status quo* had been restored in Italy. From Palmerston's point of view this was an acceptable solution. He would have preferred to have seen the Austrians retire north of the Alps and their power replaced by a strong Piedmont-Sardinia, which could have kept out the French, without the embarrassment of continual foreign interference in Italy. But, given the alternatives, a return to the old Vienna balance achieved Britain's primary objective of preventing French encroachment.

The remarkable thing was that Palmerston scored a great popular success with the British radicals as a strong supporter of Italian nationalism and liberalism. His new skill in the manipulation of public opinion seems to date from the 1847 election campaign. He was galvanized into defending his whole policy by the fact that his opponent at Tiverton was George Julian Harney, a leading Chartist and their acknowledged spokesman on foreign affairs. They met in a great set-piece debate on the hustings on 31 July in front of a very large gathering of the press. Palmerston's speech, which lasted for nearly three hours, was later published as a pamphlet. It was designed as a reply to Harney's charges that Palmerston had always really been on the side of reaction abroad, as well as at home. Harney accused him of supporting the Sultan of Turkey against the reforming Mehemet Ali, of failing to defend Cracow against the Tsar of Russia, and of helping Maria of Portugal against her own subjects who were defending the constitution, as well as of a completely immoral policy in China. Palmerston spoke brilliantly – although not always entirely truthfully – especially about Portugal. It was good-humoured, witty and an immense success with his audience. Palmerston who, even in 1847, had not entirely mastered the art of parliamentary speaking, seemed to have found his métier. In refuting Harney's charges, he had also cast himself as the great champion of European liberalism.[12] With growing confidence he repeated his Tiverton success in the House of Commons, against Thomas Anstey's rather wild accusations, in March 1848.

It was a natural development of this that the British public, and the British Court, saw him as the champion of Italian nationalism in 1848–9. The public was pleased. The Court was not; they saw his apparently anti-Austrian policy as a dangerous threat to the stability of Europe. In fact, Palmerston as well as the Court, regarded Austria as essential to the European balance of power. He argued that she would be stronger and better able to fulfil her real role in central Europe without her Italian commitments. He wrote to Leopold of the Belgians in June 1848, 'I cannot regret the expulsion of the Austrians from Italy. I do not believe, Sire, that it will diminish the real strength nor impair the real security of Austria as a European Power . . . Italy was to her the heel of Achilles, and not the shield of Ajax.' Two months later he wrote to Ponsonby in Vienna, 'North of the Alps, we wish her [Austria] all the prosperity and success in the world.'[13]

Palmerston, however, valued Austria chiefly as a counterpoise to Russia. Although he showed little sympathy with German nationalism in this period, he did express to Russell his pleasure that Prussia had broken away from Austria and 'looks to be the leading Power of independent Germany'. But Austria's ability to check Russia was severely damaged in 1849 by her need to call in Russian assistance to put down the revolution in Hungary. As Palmerston put it to Russell, 'Austria holds on to Russia for the present as a bad swimmer keeps close to a good one.'[14]

It is sometimes suggested that Palmerston showed more sympathy with the Hungarian nationalists than with the German ones because the former were impeccably aristocratic and traditionalist while the Germans were middle-class and radical. His letter to Russell of 14 September 1849 might seem to lend substance to this. He wrote, 'We ought not to . . . forget that right and justice are on the side of the Hungarians.' Although the crowns of Austria and Hungary had devolved on the same head, they were separate kingdoms. The Hungarians had the right to resist arbitrary measures from the Austrian government. 'The Hungarians', he said 'are Revolutionists in the same sense as the men to whose measures and acts at the close of the 17th century, it is owing that the present Royal Family of England, happily for the nation are seated on the Throne of these Realms.' It should, however, be remembered that this letter was intended for the Queen's eyes and presumably deployed those arguments which might be most likely to appeal to her.[15]

The immediate problem in the autumn of 1849 was that a number of leading Polish and Hungarian refugees had fled to Turkey. The Russians and Austrians demanded their return. The British ambassador in Constantinople, the formidable Stratford Canning, encouraged the Turks to refuse and Palmerston endorsed his action. The Turks, however, were reluctant to incur the wrath of Austria and Russia alone and Admiral Parker's fleet was sent to the mouth of the Dardanelles (and for a short time into the Dardanelles, in breach of the 1841 Convention). The Queen objected to this intervention, although even some conservatives held that the Turks had every right to receive the refugees if they wished to do so.

Relations between Palmerston and the Court were becoming dangerously strained. Victoria and Albert, encouraged by Baron Stockmar, had always believed that the Crown still had an active role to play in foreign affairs. In particular, the Queen disliked despatches being sent before she had seen them. This had led to trouble even during Peel's ministry but, because she liked and trusted Aberdeen, she had accepted his explanation that the prior submission of despatches was not always possible, especially when the Court was out of London. She was less ready to believe Palmerston, whom she was coming to distrust. She several times suggested to Russell that Palmerston might leave the Foreign Office and go to Ireland as Lord Lieutenant with a United Kingdom peerage, which would have given him a seat in the Lords.

Two incidents in particular caused trouble. In 1850 General Haynau, an Austrian who had been responsible for some particularly severe measures, including floggings, against the rebels, came to London. When he visited Barclays Brewery in Southwark, which was then a popular tourist attraction, he was set upon by some of the draymen and apparently tossed into a horse trough. Palmerston seems to have privately applauded their action, or at least refused to take it very seriously. He was only with difficulty persuaded to send an apology to the Austrian government. The following year, Louis Kossuth, the great Hungarian nationalist leader, came to Britain. He was accorded a hero's welcome by many people and Palmerston himself wished to meet him, but was dissuaded from doing so by the Queen and various Cabinet colleagues.

Albert and Victoria exaggerated Palmerston's hostility to Austria but they did not exaggerate the indignation which his tendency to preach both publicly and privately to European sovereigns, indeed at times to seem to try to give the law to the whole continent, was rousing among European conservatives. One clash occurred in Spain. In March 1848 he wrote to Bulwer in Madrid, advising 'the adoption of a legal and constitutional course of government', reminding the Spaniards that recent events in France had proved that even a large army was no defence for a government which put itself 'at variance with the general sentiments of the country' and recommending the inclusion of Liberals in the government. Bulwer showed the despatch to the Spanish Foreign Minister, the Duke of Sotomayor. When the Spaniards replied that they would not tolerate interference (and asked Palmerston how he would like interference in Ireland), Palmerston gave them 'a Roland for their Oliver', told them that Isabella owed her throne to British help and, without it, her ministers would have been 'proscribed exiles in a foreign land'. The Spaniards demanded that Bulwer leave within forty-eight hours. The Queen was furious both at Palmerston's tactlessness and the insult to her envoy for, she said, 'whatever way one may wish to look at it, Sir Henry is still *her* Minister'. The fault was partly Bulwer's for showing Sotomayor the despatch without clear instructions but Palmerston staunchly defended him in the Commons.[16]

A similar imbroglio occurred with Austria in November 1848. Palmerston wrote a most intemperate despatch to Vienna condemning Radetzky's actions in Milan. Radetzky had issued a proclamation which he called 'a flagrant and a palpable violation' of the truce agreed after Custozza. Even if Radetzky had not been bound by that, 'yet the moral feeling of mankind and every sentiment of generosity and justice would have been revolted against a proceeding conceived in the spirit of the most odious oppression and enunciated by doctrines which belong only to the disciples of communism, and which are subversive of the very foundations of social order'. (The reference was to possible confiscations). The new Austrian Chancellor, Schwarzenberg, replied in kind. 'Lord Palmerston', he wrote 'is a little too much inclined to consider himself the arbiter of the destinies of Europe. For our part we are not in the least disposed to attribute to him, in our own affairs, the role of providence. We never pressed on him our advice concerning the affairs of Ireland . . . I must frankly confess that we are tired of his eternal insinuations, of his tone, now protective and pedantic, now insulting, but always unbecoming and we have decided that we shall no longer tolerate it.' He said bluntly that, if Palmerston wanted war, he could have it. Palmerston secured the removal of this correspondence from the embassy archives.[17]

By this time the European conservatives were bent on destroying Palmerston. Their opportunity seemed to have arrived in 1850 when Palmerston resorted to extraordinary strong-arm measures against a small state, Greece, which was under the international protection of France and Russia, as well as Britain. Britain had genuine and long-standing grievances against the Greek government. The Greeks had repeatedly failed to pay the charges on the loan guaranteed by Britain and other Powers after Greece became independent in 1830. They had also mistreated individual Britons. A notorious, although trivial, case concerned a well-known Scottish historian, George Finlay, the garden of whose house in Athens had been seized without compensation for the building of a new royal palace.

The incident which Palmerston chose as his test case was a doubtful one. A Portuguese Jew, commonly known as Don Pacifico, had been the victim of an unpleasant anti-Semitic attack at Easter 1847, in the course of which his house had been burnt down. Failing to get redress from the Greek authorities, Don Pacifico claimed British citizenship on the grounds that he had been born in Gibraltar and asked the British government for help. What made the case dubious was the fact that Pacifico already had a reputation as a confidence trickster and, apart from the rather exaggerated value he put on his furniture, a large part of his claim for compensation rested on his assertion that papers which he needed for a lawsuit in Portugal, had also been destroyed.

Nevertheless, Palmerston decided to settle things once and for all with Greece. He told the British envoy in Greece, Thomas Wyse, in December 1849 that he had asked the Admiralty to instruct Sir William Parker 'to take in Athens on his way back from the Dardanelles, & to support you in bringing at last to a satisfactory ending the settlement of our various claims upon the Greek Govt.' Parker and Wyse were to try peaceful means first but 'If however the Greek Govt. does not strike [i.e. their colours] Parker must do so'. Parker should seize Greek property, preferably the Greek fleet if it was handy, since the government would not care about private property, and if necessary institute a blockade. He left it to Parker's discretion but added, 'I remember at one Time it was thought that a landing of Marines & sailors at some town might enable us to seize & carry off public treasure of sufficient amount. Of course Pacifico's claim must be fully satisfied.'[18] Palmerston seemed to be reliving the days of Francis Drake.

Parker duly arrived off Piraeus, the port of Athens, in January 1850 and established a blockade. Britain's co-guarantors of Greece, France and Russia, protested at this unilateral action and the French offered to mediate. Palmerston, under pressure from his Cabinet colleagues, accepted the French mediation. At first he was inclined to instruct Wyse to take a very stiff line. They must have money, not promises. 'The word of the Greek Govt, is as good as its Bond, and the Bondholders can tell us what that is worth.' He hoped that Wyse would have taken the opportunity to occupy Cervi and Sapienza, two islands in dispute between Greece and the Ionian Islands, then a British Protectorate.[19] But Palmerston's confidence and claims began to deflate. He became suspicious of Pacifico's and even Finlay's estimates. In March he had reduced his immediate demands to less than £2,000 – £500 for Pacifico (he had claimed over £5,000), £750 for Finlay and £420 for various minor claims. The Greeks, he suggested, could hardly say they could not pay that. As to any demand upon the British government by merchant captains whose vessels had been seized, 'our answer would be "we wish you may get it"'.[20]

In April a compromise agreement was reached in London between Palmerston and the Greek and French ambassadors but in the meanwhile Wyse, acting on out-of-date orders, had reimposed the blockade on Piraeus and the Greeks yielded to the original British demands. The French recalled their ambassador from London.

Almost everyone in a position to know the facts thought that Palmerston had gone much too far this time. The so-called Don Pacifico debate in June 1850 was in fact a concerted conservative attack on the whole of what they saw as Palmerston's provocative and irresponsible policy since 1847. Aberdeen and Stanley (later Earl of Derby) led the attack in the Lords. Aberdeen concentrated on the activities of Parker's fleet. Apart from the blockade of Athens, it had encouraged the Sicilians, then abandoned them to their fate and it had unnecessarily broken the 1841 Straits Convention. He also echoed the continental charges of the British double standard of political morality. There had been risings in the Ionian Islands too in 1848–9. The British had suppressed them as severely as the Austrians had done in Italy, even resorting to floggings. (Parker's fleet was popularly, but mistakenly, supposed to have brought the cat o' nine tails). There was much truth in all these charges, and there was some in the even graver

charge that, by encouraging the Italians, Palmerston had so weakened
Austria that the Austrians had been reduced to dependence on the Russians
– an outcome which conservatives and liberals alike deplored. At any rate
the House of Lords was convinced and Palmerston's policy condemned by
169 votes to 132.

The debate now moved to the House of Commons. By prior
arrangement the radical, J.A. Roebuck, moved a motion on 24 June
praising Palmerston, and the debate lasted four days. Peel, who had
previously refrained from attacking Palmerston's policy even though he
disapproved of it, because he wanted the Russell government to remain in
power for domestic reasons, now launched a strong attack. He represented
his and Aberdeen's policy as the sane alternative to Palmerston's
adventuring. Palmerston knew that he was fighting for his political life.

He responded in one of the greatest speeches of his life, ranging over his
whole policy from Minto's mission onwards. Defending his actions in Italy
and elsewhere, he claimed that they had always been in support of
moderate reform and, above all, patriotic and in England's interests. But
he scored his greatest success on what was really his weakest point, his
defence of Don Pacifico. He ended with the famous peroration 'as the
Roman, in days of old, held himself free from indignity when he could say
civis Romanus sum; so also a British subject, in whatever land he may be,
shall feel confident that the watchful eye and strong arm of England will
protect him against injustice and wrong'. The public loved it. Gladstone
might protest that the Roman citizen was the member of a privileged caste,
enjoying rights denied to the rest of the world and ask 'Is such, then, the
view of the noble Lord, as to the relation that is to subsist between England
and other countries?'[21] Palmerston might have answered 'Yes'; the man in
the street would almost certainly have done so.

His fellow MPs were not quite so sure. Palmerston secured his vote of
confidence with a majority of 46 because the government could hardly do
other than rally to the support of their own Foreign Secretary. But Russell
and other members of the Cabinet were beginning to share the Court's
opinion that Palmerston was a dangerous man, who would be better
removed from the Foreign Office. Russell's opportunity to act came over
France.

Palmerston's attitude to France, where the greatest danger to European
peace lay, had always been extremely cautious. He shared the general fear
that French republics tended to be adventurous in their foreign policy and
he particularly resented links between the French and the Irish rebels. At
the same time Britain had no real alternative to accepting the *fait accompli*

of a French republic in February 1848 and he played his usual game of trying to influence French policy by co-operation, rather than confrontation. This underlay most of his Italian policy. In an interesting discussion with Russell in April 1849, he expressed the opinion that Britain must in the last resort ally herself with France rather than Austria. She could thus restrain France and, hopefully, 'control' Austria and Russia. If she opted for Austria she might lose France, without gaining Austria (because of Austrian dependence on Russia) and he added significantly, they would not gain a single Tory vote at home by doing so.[22]

When Louis Bonaparte, the nephew of the great emperor, was legally elected President of the French republic in December 1848, Palmerston like many Englishmen had mixed feelings. It seemed to promise an end to the extremism and upheavals in Paris but would Bonaparte now feel compelled to embark on a 'glorious' foreign policy which would threaten British interests? On 2 December 1851 Bonaparte carried out his *coup d'état,* dissolving the National Assembly, arresting leading republicans and paving the way for the extension of his own term as President, which would otherwise have ended in 1852. Palmerston believed that he acted to forestall an Orleanist plot.[23] The British Cabinet agreed to adopt a neutral attitude for the time being but on 3 December Palmerston told Walewski, the French ambassador in London, (who was himself reputedly an illegitimate son of Napoleon I), that he approved of the President's prompt action. The British ambassador in Paris, Lord Normanby, who disliked both Bonaparte and Palmerston, complained that he had been placed in an impossible position.

Russell decided that the moment had come to act. He again offered Palmerston the Lord Lieutenancy of Ireland and a United Kingdom peerage. When Palmerston refused, he asked for his resignation. There was a surge of indignation in the press. The *Morning Advertiser* asked 'Will Englishmen submit to this? Are they prepared tamely to acquiesce in seeing the most able, the most energetic, the most generous-minded, the most *English* Minister that ever presided over the Foreign Affairs of this country, "barely" sacrificed to the despotic Courts of the Continent?' Palmerston received letters of sympathy from people in all walks of life. The Mayor of Southampton wanted to know why 'our Minister, I mean the People's Minister is dismissed'.[24]

When Parliament reassembled in February 1852 Radicals asked the same question. Russell, in Palmerston's opinion, behaved very improperly by bringing before the House the latter's disputes with Victoria about the sending of despatches – improperly because Palmerston could scarcely answer them without dragging the Crown into politics. But, more devastating to Palmerston's radical support, were the revelations about his approval of Louis Napoleon's *coup d'état*. Palmerston did not reply effectively and Disraeli, for one, thought he was finished for good. But Disraeli underestimated him. Less than a month later he had his 'tit-for-tat with John Russell' when he joined with the Tory opposition to defeat Russell on his Militia Bill, on the grounds that it was inadequate to provide for national defence. Russell resigned. Palmerston was free to become a maverick force in domestic politics, as some believed he already was in foreign politics.

7

Home Secretary in the Aberdeen Coalition

After the great clash between Palmerston and the Conservatives in June 1850, nothing must have seemed more unlikely than that Palmerston would join a coalition government led by his principal rival, Aberdeen, in December 1852. But the early 1850s were a strange time in British politics. The break up of the Conservative party after Peel's repeal of the Corn Laws in the summer of 1846 had left Lord Stanley as the leader of the Protectionists, who formed the largest single party in the Commons. Lord Stanley did not succeed his father as Earl of Derby until 1851 but had gone to the Lords as Baron Stanley in 1844, and the Protectionists in the Commons had no obvious leader. Virtually all the men of talent in the Commons (as well as in the Lords) had gone out with Peel. Benjamin Disraeli, the only really able man left among the Protectionists in the Commons, was without ministerial experience and as yet unacceptable as party leader.

Russell could command an overall majority in the Commons so long as he could keep his rather unwieldy coalition of Whigs, Radicals and Irish together but it was a difficult balancing act and Russell's temper grew short. He offered his resignation to the Queen in February 1851 after a minor defeat. A premature attempt was made to put together a new Whig-Peelite coalition and, after Stanley too had failed to form a government, Russell returned to office with a Whig administration in March 1851. By now, new political alignments were being freely canvassed. Russell had mortally offended his Irish Catholic supporters by putting through the Ecclesiastical Titles Act of 1850, aimed at preventing the resumption of territorial titles by Roman Catholic bishops in England. He had also lost the confidence of many Whigs, for reasons which even contemporaries found it rather hard to explain. It was not too difficult for Palmerston to secure Russell's overthrow on the Militia Bill in February 1852. This time Derby did succeed in forming an administration. In the election held in the summer of 1852, the Derbyites increased their numbers in the Commons from 280 to 310. The election was so corrupt and there was so much resort to violence that it dismayed even a public well-accustomed to both. But it had still not produced a party with an overall majority in the Commons.

Intermittent discussions continued between the Whigs and the Peelites. Parliamentary reform, intended to prevent any repetition of the events of 1852, was one plank in the programme. There was, however, a groundswell of opinion among the conservative-minded, who included both Whigs and Protectionists, to stop any further reform of parliament. One idea was the so-called 'Lansdowne project' to bring the elderly Lord Lansdowne out of retirement to head a ministry which would resist any 'disfranchising' Reform Bill and instead to bring in one which 'shall have the semblance of change with the minimum of reality'. It was hoped that such a scheme would 'entrain' a large proportion of the Whig aristocracy and many of Lord Derby's supporters.[1]

Russell's brother, the Duke of Bedford, told Sir James Graham, a leading Peelite, early in August 1852 that Palmerston had opened negotiations to place Lansdowne at the head of such a coalition government, making it clear that he, Palmerston, would serve with Russell but not under him. Early in October, Palmerston made direct overtures to Lansdowne. In a letter from Broadlands, he once again poured out his indignation at Russell's treatment of him and denounced Russell as 'not to be depended upon . . . infirm of purpose, changeable in his views'. In particular, he denounced Russell's apparent change of views on the franchise question. In the autumn of 1851 he, Palmerston, had agreed to 'a moderate extension of the Franchise' but now Russell was talking of a measure which would disfranchise, not fourteen, but nearly eighty boroughs. He repeated that he would never serve under Russell but would serve on equal terms with him under a third person. He made it clear that he thought that third person must be Lansdowne. Lansdowne resisted Palmerston's pressure. He did not believe that 'amidst all the jealousies which I see prevailing' he could re-unite the party.[2]

The Lansdowne project was not the only iron that Palmerston had in the fire. Bedford had also told Graham that relations between Palmerston and Gladstone, who was then still an opponent of further parliamentary reform, were becoming very intimate. Even more startling was the growing alliance between Palmerston and Disraeli, again based on opposition to parliamentary reform. Disraeli seems to have made the first overture when he wrote to Palmerston's *confidant,* Peter Borthwick, the proprietor of the *Morning Post,* in December 1851 expressing his 'surprise and indignation at the ingratitude of [Palmerston's] colleagues'.[3] Graham thought that a Palmerston-Disraeli coalition might well command a majority in the House of Commons. Derby himself was conscious of the need for a good and experienced Foreign Secretary to strengthen his ministry. At first he thought that he would be able to lure Aberdeen back to the main body of the Conservative party but, when that attempt failed, he made overtures to Palmerston.[4] Palmerston, however, declined to take either the Foreign or Home Office from Derby. Ashley rightly said that the Protectionists, almost leaderless in the Commons, looked to Palmerston as a medieval Italian state looked to an unemployed *condottiere* of good repute to lead them.[5] But it was not to be.

Derby's government was brought down in December 1852 on the question of Disraeli's budget. The way was open for the formation of the Whig-Peelite coalition under Aberdeen. On 21 December Aberdeen asked Palmerston whether he would join it. Palmerston at first replied that they had 'stood so long in hostile array one against the other, that it was too late now to join'. He did not think the combination would be acceptable to either party and he saw the fact that the new administration would be committed to parliamentary reform as an insuperable obstacle to his joining. Rather surprisingly, Palmerston changed his mind the next day and sent a carefully worded message through Lord Lansdowne, indicating that he would be available if asked. An equally carefully worded message went back through Lord Lansdowne, offering him the Home Office. Palmerston accepted.[6]

The inclusion of Palmerston caused something of a sensation. Graham wrote in his diary, 'There is no room for Disraeli and Lord Derby. Otherwise we had better all kiss and be friends at once.' The Queen and Prince Albert also had misgivings. Aberdeen assured them that he and Palmerston were, to quote the Prince's memorandum, 'great friends (!!!) of sixty years' standing, having been at school together'. The Prince added, 'We could not help laughing heartily at the *Harrow* Boys and their friendship.'[7] In fact, no one doubted that Palmerston had been invited in because he would have been too dangerous left outside. The Derbyites were still the largest party in the Commons. If Palmerston and Disraeli combined to lead them, as still seemed very possible, they could probably have brought down any government.

Aberdeen was not being entirely disingenuous in assuring the Queen that he and Palmerston remained friends. They had disagreed bitterly about the conduct of foreign affairs from 1848 to 1850 but their personal relations were seldom bad and most members of the coalition were quite happy to sit in Cabinet with Palmerston so long as he was kept out of the Foreign Office. Palmerston himself seems to have realized that he had made too many enemies for a return to the Foreign Office to be practical and, in the various negotiations earlier in the year, had indicated that the Home Office would interest him.

Palmerston threw himself into his work at the Home Office with his accustomed energy but he was not, as he is sometimes represented, ploughing a lonely reforming furrow. The whole coalition was potentially a great reforming ministry, containing almost every first-rate political talent of the period. From the beginning, as both Gladstone and the Duke of Argyll testified, they acted together as a remarkably homogenous team on most domestic issues despite their diverse political origins. Palmerston said much the same thing to his brother.[8] Aberdeen himself, the disciple of William Pitt and friend of Robert Peel, was not at all afraid of practical reform. Their initial reforming programme ranged widely from Gladstone's attempt to introduce an entirely new fiscal and economic strategy to a comprehensive scheme to reform education at all levels from the ancient universities of Oxford and Cambridge to the financing of elementary schools.

Palmerston's work at the Home Office fitted snugly into this general framework. It was extremely practical, in some ways reminiscent of his work at the War Office at the beginning of his career, and Palmerston was luckier than many of his colleagues in that much of it was embodied in legislation before the whole government programme was aborted once and for all by the Crimean War. It related to three main areas, penal reform, factory legislation and public health.

Penal reform was partly forced on the government by the refusal of most of the Australian colonies to receive any more transported criminals but the whole transportation system had been under debate since the 1830s. Palmerston was lobbied both by the penal reformers, who wanted to humanize the system, and by the 'law and order' party, who were dismayed by what they saw as the public disorders of the 1840s and early 1850s. The centre piece of the new legislation was the Penal Servitude Act of 1853, which substituted imprisonment for transportation. But it was recognized that confinement at home would often be more onerous than transportation to the colonies, where many convicts had enjoyed considerable freedom under a ticket-of-leave, or parole, system. A similar parole system was therefore for the first time introduced at home.

Palmerston was influenced by the thinking of contemporary reformers, especially on the treatment of young offenders. He visited Parkhurst prison on the Isle of Wight, a special institution set up for young offenders in 1838, and characteristically recommended practical improvements to the ventilation of the cells. He was also responsible for the Youthful Offenders Act which allowed the transfer of young offenders from prison to reform schools. His support for the use of solitary confinement in prisons would be less acceptable to modern taste but in mid-Victorian times it was regarded as a useful means of preventing the corruption of the comparatively innocent by the hardened criminal. He was compelled by public pressure to make hard labour regimes in prisons even harsher than they already were.

He first became interested in factory reform in the 1840s. Two strong-minded and ingenious trade unionists, Philip Grant and Benjamin Haworth, called on him one afternoon to lobby his support for the Ten Hours Bill. Palmerston was at first dismissive, telling them, 'Oh, the work of the children cannot be so hard as you represent it, as I am led to understand that the machinery does all the work without the aid of the children, attention to the spindles only being required'. Grant then had the idea of a practical demonstration. He and Haworth seized two large arm chairs and pushed them back and forth across the room on their castors to simulate the action of the looms which the children had to tend. Palmerston himself joined in the game with gusto and emerged finally convinced of the truth of what his son-in-law, Shaftesbury, had told him of the exhausting nature of factory work.[9]

He voted for the Ten Hours Bill in 1844 but his approach in 1853 was cautious. Shaftesbury wanted a far-reaching measure, limiting the hours of women and certain other groups. Palmerston declined to 'interfere by legislation' with the right of those of full age 'to work as long or as little as they think fit'. But he did introduce a Bill to forbid the employment of children between 6 p.m. and 6 a.m. Although this was primarily intended to close a loophole in the existing law relating to children, it had an effect on adult workers too since many operations depended on the presence of child workers.

Public health legislation was also to some extent forced on the government by the continuing prevalence of cholera. Palmerston's papers include elaborate plans, some of which were carried out, for a new sewerage system for London which would allow the effluent to be discharged in the Thames, downstream of the capital. He also kept, although perhaps as a curiosity, a remarkable scheme for transforming sewage into fertiliser, 'British Guano', in caverns beneath the capital, to be staffed by convicts. The 'Guano' would be sent to the countryside in the empty railway trucks which had brought coal to London. More seriously, he successfully brought in a Smoke Abatement Bill, in an attempt to curb the notorious London 'pea-soupers', or smogs as a later generation would call them. He would, he told his brother, try to 'compel the tall chimneys to burn their own smoke'.[10]

Despite the unhappy experience of his own family he supported the measure which made it compulsory for all infants to be vaccinated against smallpox. This roused considerable opposition in some quarters. So did the legislation he brought in to end burials under church floors and to require all burials in future to take place in church yards or public cemeteries. This caused strong indignation among some clergy which drew from Palmerston the tart rebuke that he saw no special connection 'between church dignitaries and the privilege of being decomposed under the feet of the survivors'. He had another skirmish with the devout when the presbytery of Edinburgh asked the government to proclaim a day of fasting and humiliation for the ending of a cholera epidemic there. Palmerston replied, in effect, that heaven helped those who helped themselves and that the citizens of Edinburgh could hardly expect divine intervention on their behalf until they did something about their over-crowded tenements.[11]

Palmerston caused offence to the religious-minded on a number of counts. His allowing separate plots for Catholics and Dissenters in the new public cemeteries did not please the established Church, nor did his ending of the Anglican monopoly of gaol chaplaincies. At the same time, Palmerston still had some sympathy with the spirit of Russell's Ecclesiastical Titles Act and would have liked to have prevented Catholic monks and nuns from appearing publicly in their religious habits but the Prime Minister dissuaded him from such intolerance. Palmerston's oddest quarrel with the devout arose from a speech he made to a labourers' meeting at Romsey in the winter of 1854, when he expressed the opinion that all children were born good and that only bad education or associations corrupted them. He was accused of denying the doctrine of original sin.

But Palmerston was a practical man and he believed that the control of the environment could do a great deal to improve society. Not all his measures were popular with the working classes, particularly his attack on the 'Beer Shops' where, he said, the labouring classes interpreted the phrase 'licensed to be drunk, on the Premises', as applying to the customers as well as the beer. 'They are' he complained, 'the Haunts of Thieves and Schools of Prostitutes. They demoralize the lower Classes'.[12]

But while Palmerston undoubtedly wanted to improve the material environment of the workers, his whole policy was permeated with a fear of the untamed tiger of the working classes, particularly if they were organized by the trade unions. A Bill was introduced into the Commons in 1853 which would have legalised peaceful picketing. Palmerston opposed it, although he was prepared to re-affirm the 1826 measure which permitted men to withdraw their labour in an industrial dispute. Peaceful picketing, he said, would stop poor men from working for very low wages if they wished to do so to save their families from starving.

As Home Secretary, Palmerston was responsible for the detection and control of subversion and here his responsibilities brought him very close to his old field of foreign affairs. There was an assassination attempt against the Emperor of Austria in February 1853, followed by new disturbances in northern Italy. The Austrians believed that both were instigated by Kossuth and Mazzini and had been planned in England by a mysterious body known as the 'London Committee'. In April Palmerston received information that Kossuth was negotiating to buy arms from an English arms manufacturer, a Mr Hain, who had a factory at Rotherhithe. The police were unable to find firm evidence to connect Kossuth with Hain and the latter was eventually prosecuted for merely technical offences under the Explosives Act of 1836.

By now, however, the case had become a *cause célèbre. The Times* led a press campaign, demanding action against foreign revolutionaries who abused British hospitality. Various foreign governments were making the same demands at the diplomatic level. The Radicals meanwhile pressed Palmerston to explain himself in the Commons. How had the police come to take an interest in Hain's perfectly legal factory in the first place? It became obvious that Kossuth and other refugees were under police surveillance. The Radicals almost begged Palmerston to dissociate himself from the matter and blame the Chief Commissioner of the Metropolitan police but Palmerston accepted full responsibility and gave more offence by refusing to clear Kossuth's name publicly, despite the lack of evidence.[13] The contrast with 1850 could hardly have been more stark.

Palmerston would probably never have recovered his popularity with the Radicals but for the Eastern Question. One reason why he had been willing to go to the Home Office in 1852 was that it would still leave him in a position to concentrate on the reform of the militia. Palmerston was deeply and seriously concerned about the defence of the country. In this he was in no way at odds with the Prime Minister. Aberdeen had resisted re-armament in the 1840s because he did not believe that the France of Louis Philippe represented any threat to Britain. By contrast, both he and Palmerston considered that the France of Napoleon III represented a very real threat. Sooner or later Napoleon III would have to establish his credibility with his own people by showing himself the true heir of the great Napoleon.

The British public was in an unwontedly belligerent mood. It was almost as if the excitement which had led to the revolutions in continental Europe in 1848–9 had been dammed back in Britain and, in the early 1850s, ran in other channels. There was more industrial unrest in Britain in this period than is usually realized. There were cotton strikes in the north of England and, to the beleaguered upper classes, in the capital, everyone from cab drivers to policemen seemed to be threatening strike action. But, for the most part, the malaise sought a foreign enemy.

The House of Commons, usually so parsimonious about the Service estimates, almost forced money on the government. Palmerston wrote to Aberdeen that he did not think war would come immediately but Napoleon was 'working hard to place himself in such a Position of relative strength as to enable him to strike a stunning Blow whenever a dispute may arise, or whenever it may suit his purpose to do so'. Parliament might be less willing to vote money in the future. They should therefore spend the extra money, not on men but on permanent installations, dockyards, harbours of refuge, the steam engine factory at Plymouth and fortifications of the Channel Islands.[14] All this would have been an admirable precaution against the expected blow from France. It was totally useless in the war in which they actually found themselves engaged against Russia.

It was Napoleon III, not the Tsar Nicholas, who first threw down the gauntlet in the Eastern Mediterranean. In February 1852 the Sultan conceded most of the Latin Church's claims over the Holy Places in Jerusalem and elsewhere which Napoleon, anxious to conciliate the clerical party in France, had been pressing since 1850. In May 1852 Napoleon sent the French ambassador, Charles Lavalette, to Constantinople aboard a powerful warship, the *Charlemagne*. Although technically allowable under the Convention of 1841, the action was generally regarded as a breach of its spirit. In February 1853 the Tsar responded by sending Prince Menshikov to Constantinople. He assured the British government, and Aberdeen believed him, that he only wished to insist that the Turks must observe their existing treaties with Russia, especially those related to the rights of the Orthodox Church.

Palmerston's reaction was sharper than that of the Prime Minister. It has been held by both contemporaries and historians that the Crimean War could have been avoided if either Aberdeen or Palmerston's policies had been consistently followed, and this analysis is probably correct. There is no evidence that the Tsar wanted war with Turkey or that he was planning a forward move on Constantinople at this time. His conversations with the British ambassador, Sir Hamilton Seymour, in January 1853, although they looked so sinister in retrospect, were almost certainly only part of the contingency planning which had been going on between the Powers for twenty years on what they would do if the Ottoman empire did collapse despite their attempts to preserve it. Palmerston, throughout this period, believed that, if the British government took a strong line and warned the Tsar by fleet movements that Britain would resist any forward move, Russia would retreat from a confrontation. Aberdeen, at first seeing the Tsar's actions as a rational response to a French challenge, argued that fleet movements would escalate the situation and make a peaceful settlement harder to achieve.

Lavalette responded to the Menshikov mission by summoning a French fleet to the Eastern Mediterranean. Colonel Rose, the British chargé d'affaires in Constantinople, sent a similar request to Admiral Dundas at Malta but Dundas refused to move without orders from London. The Cabinet supported Sir James Graham, the First Lord of the Admiralty, in refusing Rose's request and Lord Clarendon, the Foreign Secretary, rebuked the French for listening to 'rumours' and 'gossip'. Palmerston acquiesced at this time.

The situation changed in May. The formidable Stratford Canning, now Lord Stratford de Redcliffe, arrived back in Constantinople early in April. By his good offices the original dispute about the Holy Places was quickly settled but on 5 May Menshikov presented the Turks with what was virtually an ultimatum, demanding that they agree to a new Convention. The Turks refused and Menshikov left Constantinople on 22 May. The problem about the new Convention was that it could be interpreted either as a vague reiteration of Russia's existing treaty rights or as a new and startling claim on the part of Russia to exercise a virtual protectorate over Turkey's twelve million Orthodox subjects.

This was the point at which Aberdeen and Palmerston's views began to diverge. Aberdeen saw no reason to believe that Nicholas's intentions were not still limited and peaceful. Palmerston had begun to champion the Turkish empire in a way which the Prime Minister thought quite unrealistic. Palmerston, with the co-operation of Stratford Canning, had tried hard in the 1840s to compel the Turks to reform themselves. He now professed to believe that the reforms had worked and that they were now dealing with a state which was in many ways more civilized than Russia. The Turkish commercial system was more liberal, he argued; there was more religious toleration; almost all the inhabitants of the Ottoman empire were free, unlike the Russian serfs; personal liberty was more secure and the press was freer. Aberdeen, who had travelled in Turkey, did not believe a word of it. He would, he said, as soon think of preferring the Koran to the Bible 'as of comparing the Christianity and civilization of Russia to the fanaticism & immorality of the Turks'.[15]

Of more immediate moment was the fact that, by the end of May 1853, Palmerston was arguing strongly for the sending of a British fleet to the Bosporus, even though this would be a clear breach of the Treaty of 1841. Aberdeen objected not only because it would be a breach of treaty but because, when exactly the same issue had arisen during the Russo-Turkish war in 1829, Wellington himself had resisted such a move on the grounds that the British fleet could be too easily cut off. But both Clarendon, the Foreign Secretary, and Russell, the Leader of the House of Commons, were beginning to side with Palmerston. At their meeting on 4 June, the Cabinet agreed to send the fleet to Besika Bay, outside the Dardanelles, and to give Stratford authority to summon it to Constantinople if he felt it to be necessary.

Early in July 1853 the Russians occupied the principalities of Moldavia and Wallachia at the mouth of the Danube (the modern Roumania). The British Cabinet held that this was a *casus belli* to which the Turks could properly have responded by declaring war, but they exerted all their influence to persuade the Turks to wait until a, by now thoroughly alarmed, Europe had tried what diplomacy could do. At the beginning of August it seemed that the matter had been peacefully settled. The Great Powers had agreed a compromise solution, the Vienna Note, drawn up by an ambassadorial conference in the Austrian capital, and the Russians had accepted it. On 20 August the Turks rejected the Vienna Note and put forward an alternative proposal. British sympathy for the Turks began to evaporate but the situation was changed yet again by a famous 'leak' in a German newspaper in September, revealing that the Russians had apparently been interpreting the Vienna Note in a quite different sense from anyone else and saw it as an admission of the most extreme of Menshikov's claims.

From then on, it was difficult to resist Palmerston's insistence that only strong language and strong actions would deter the Tsar. It was in fact

Aberdeen and Clarendon who on 23 September instructed Stratford to summon the fleet to Constantinople, nominally to protect foreign nationals. Palmerston was contemptuous of this transparent excuse which, he said, would not deceive the Russians – although it may not have been entirely an excuse in view of the war fever in Constantinople, which compelled the Turkish government to declare war on Russia in the first week of October.

On 7 October Palmerston sent Aberdeen a clear statement of what he felt should be done. Britain and France should conclude a convention with the Sultan promising him such assistance as he might require, and allow British and French subjects wishing to do so to enter his service. More than that, they should instruct their squadrons to enter the Black Sea 'and should send word to the Russian admiral at Sebastopol that in the existing state of things any Russian ship of war found cruising in the Black Sea would be detained, and given over to the Turkish government'. The Cabinet which met later that day was not prepared to go as far as that. In the end they agreed to Clarendon's proposal that the fleet should enter the Black Sea only if the Russians attacked the Turkish coast or crossed the Danube.[16]

All was not yet lost. The Tsar had in effect assured the other Powers that, despite the Turkish declaration of war, he would do nothing to escalate the conflict until it was clear that all the diplomatic initiatives, which were still going on, had failed. That was why the so-called 'massacre' of Sinope was so important. It seems to have been, as the Russians claimed, an accident rather like the battle of Navarino a quarter of a century earlier. A Russian squadron, looking for ships which were running guns to rebels in the Caucasus, came across a Turkish fleet in Sinope Bay. Shots were fired in confused circumstances; the battle became general and the Turkish fleet annihilated. But to the government in London it looked as if the Tsar had done exactly what he had led them to believe he would not do – authorized a descent on the Turkish coast. News of Sinope reached London on 12 December. The situation envisaged at the Cabinet of 7 October seemed to have arisen.

Ironically, Palmerston was absent from the Cabinets which took the vital decisions at the end of December. There is no reason to doubt that he had resigned on a domestic issue, parliamentary reform. He was speaking the truth when he told Lansdowne that popular opinion was wrong in thinking that he had resigned on the Eastern Question; on the contrary, it was the delicate state of the Eastern Question which had made him hesitate because he believed that he was at last winning the Cabinet battle there.

Palmerston had made it clear before he joined the Coalition that parliamentary reform might well be his sticking point. The question had been postponed from the 1853 to the 1854 session, mainly because of the pressure of other business such as Gladstone's Budget, but also because it was known to be controversial within the Cabinet. Every attempt had been made to conciliate Palmerston and he had been invited to join the special Cabinet committee considering the issue but he told Aberdeen on 10 December that he would resign if there were not fundamental changes in the measure.

There is no doubting the strength of Palmerston's feelings, although they seem to have hardened over the previous eighteen months. He had told Derby during their discussions in February 1852, 'I thought that seeing that Education and Intelligence were increasing among the lower classes we might without inconvenience let out a Reef in our Franchise.' He felt that an £8 franchise in the boroughs (instead of £10) would be acceptable but £5 would be too low.[17] His increasing obstinacy seems to be connected with his almost pathological fear of the working classes and the trade unions which was developing at this time. He wrote to Aberdeen a little later that a reduction to £6 would admit 150,000 additional voters who would be 'poor, ignorant and dependent'. He went on

> Everybody who knows anything about the working classes will tell you that they are not free agents. The system or organisation which universally prevails among them by means of the Trade Unions gives to their agitating leaders an absolute despotism over the masses. This has been abundantly proved by the recent strikes. The strikers are compelled to refuse to work at a certain Rate of wage on the Pretence that those wages are not enough to support them with the present Price of Things; and yet other men at work at those very Rates, are compelled to contribute a Portion of those wages towards the support of those who are idle and earning nothing. These six Pound voters will on the one Hand be coerced by their Leaders to vote for Chartist, or ultra-Radical Candidates; and on the other Hand will be urged by their employers to vote for some other Person. They will be between the Hammer and the anvil like the Irish peasant . . . Can it be expected that men who murder their children to get 9£ to be spent in drink will not sell their vote for whatever they can get for it?[18]

The next logical step would be a demand for the secret ballot. The sincerity of Palmerston's opposition to the secret ballot is proved beyond doubt by his letter to Russell after he had lost the South Hampshire seat in 1835. He realized that his defeat was largely due to the dependence of voters on Tory landlords and believed that a secret ballot would have guaranteed him a large majority. He still called it an 'absurd Plan', however, and added 'But exceptional advantages cannot counterbalance inherent objections'.[19]

In December 1853 the Queen was delighted to hear of his resignation, especially on 'unpopular ground', which would expose him to the condemnation of 'his former Radical Admirers'.[20] Palmerston, however, was having second thoughts. He had not received the support he expected in the Cabinet, especially from Lord Lansdowne, and he wrote again to Aberdeen on 23 December, suggesting that there had been a misunderstanding. His resignation had been contingent on his belief that further amendments to the Bill were no longer possible. He now knew that this was not the case. Aberdeen, although sceptical as to how Palmerston, being on the Cabinet committee himself, could have misunderstood, accepted the withdrawal of his resignation.

Before he left the Cabinet early in December, Palmerston had made his views on the Eastern Question clear. He sent a long letter to Aberdeen on 10 December, urging that a combined British, French and Turkish fleet should enter the Black Sea. 'In the Black Sea', he wrote 'the combined English, French and Turkish squadrons were indisputably superior to the Russian fleet . . . What I would strongly recommend, therefore, is that which I proposed some months ago to the Cabinet, namely, that the Russian Government and the Russian admiral at Sebastopol should be informed that, so long as Russian troops occupy the Principalities or hold a position in any other part of the Turkish territory, no Russian ship of war can be allowed to show itself out of port in the Black Sea.' It would be objected that this was an act of hostility towards Russia but so was the declaration to which the Cabinet had already agreed that they would not tolerate a Russian attack on the Turkish coast.[21]

It is most unlikely that the Cabinet would have agreed to Palmerston's proposal but for the news of Sinope. The French had already decided to act as Palmerston had suggested in his letter of 10 December. The long and confused Cabinet meeting of 22 December, at which Palmerston was not present, felt that they had no alternative but to align their policy with that of France.

The decision was officially communicated to the Russian government on 11 January. The initial Russian reaction was surprisingly mild. They merely asked whether the Turks had also been asked to give a similar undertaking to keep their fleet in port. When they did not receive a satisfactory reply, they withdrew their ambassadors from London and

Paris early in February. Towards the end of that month Britain and France demanded the Russian troops be withdrawn from the Principalities. When the Russians refused, Britain declared war on 28 March 1854.

8

The Crimean War and the Premiership

The British public is rarely excited by questions of foreign policy. The Crimean War was one of the great exceptions. Before, as well as during, the war, the public was in a state of febrile excitement. By the late-nineteenth century it had come to seem obvious to some historians that the Crimean War had been fought about the defence of India and the route to India. There is an element of hindsight in this, a reading back of the pivotal importance of Egypt after the opening of the Suez Canal in 1869. In the eyes of contemporaries the war was fought at least as much about the balance of power in Europe, in particular about the role of Russia.

The Indian dimension did exist. Since the 1820s there had been those who had been warning the government that Russia represented the greatest future threat to Britain's Indian empire. At this time the threat was perceived mainly in terms of a Russian advance which would menace the north-west frontier, the traditional invasion route to the sub-continent. Canning had taken a relaxed attitude to the Russo-Persian war of 1826 but Wellington was alarmed by the Russian victory over Turkey in 1828–9, which had culminated in the treaty of Adrianople and Russia's acquisition of further territory on the eastern shore of the Black Sea. In the 1830s Palmerston came to share Wellington's alarm. The most vigorous British counter-measure, the pre-emptive strike against Afghanistan in 1838, met with mixed success. By 1842 Britain had withdrawn again. But by 1849 both Sind and the Punjab had been annexed. Palmerston himself was of the opinion that when 'the man from Caucasus and the man from Calcutta' met in Central Asia, it should be as far as possible from the heartland of British India. In this sense anything that happened in the sprawling Ottoman empire was of vital interest to Britain.[1]

But Kingsley Martin is entirely correct in saying that India featured very little in the memoirs, the diplomatic documents or, perhaps surprisingly, the propaganda of the period.[2] The Tsar was the bogy man of Europe for quite a different reason: in 1832 the radical, Joseph Hume, had called him 'a monster in human form'. It had been Russian actions in Poland in particular which had continually roused radical anger in both Britain and France. The Radicals had not been able to do anything to help the Poles but there had begun a remarkable identification of the Polish cause with that of the oppressed at home. In 1831 the *Westminster Review* even proclaimed, 'If the Russians are driven over the Niemen, we shall have the ballot.' These feelings were intensified by the Russian intervention in Hungary in 1849 and found public expression in the hero's welcome given to Kossuth in Britain. Russophobia was incarnated in the near-lunatic hostility of David Urquhart, who combined it with such personal hostility to Palmerston (who had sacked him from the only diplomatic post he had ever held, as First Secretary at Constantinople) that he believed Palmerston to be a secret agent of the Tsar. In August 1840 he wrote a memorandum for Melbourne accusing Palmerston of high treason. A copy survives among the Broadlands papers with a gleeful docket in Palmerston's own hand, 'A copy of this was sent to each Cabinet Minister. The letters were left in the morning at the Door of the F.O. to be laid on the Table in the Cabinet Room. The Cabinet was to meet that Day on Syrian affairs.'[3] No one believed in Palmerston's treason but it is a measure of popular hysteria that for a time in the late 1840s and early 1850s Urquhart's belief that Russia embodied 'all evil' in Europe for a time commanded general assent among the public.[4]

Palmerston, like many other politicians of the period, had close ties with the press. He gave friendly journalists inside information and sometimes drafted articles himself. His link with the *Morning Chronicle* was broken in 1848 when it was acquired by the Peelites but, about the same time, Peter Borthwick, who now owned the *Morning Post,* struck up an alliance with Palmerston. Peter Borthwick died in 1852 but his son, Algernon, who succeeded him, was even more of an enthusiast for Palmerston's policies than his father had been.[5]

No other paper had the same kind of personal connection with Palmerston that the *Morning Post* enjoyed although he also fed information into other smaller papers like the *Globe.* He was fortunate, however, in gaining the support of a number of Whig and Radical papers, ranging from the *Morning Advertiser* to the *Daily News.* The *Morning Advertiser* was an extraordinary but influential journal, with a circulation second only to *The Times*. It was taken by practically every publican in the country, because it ran an insurance scheme for them, and Palmerston's pugnacious style exactly suited the subscribers and their customers. Even Tory papers like the *Morning Herald* and Disraeli's newly-founded, *The Press,* veered to supporting Palmerston's policy against Aberdeen's supposed 'appeasement'. They propagated the view that Palmerston's resignation in December 1853 had really been on the Eastern Question and that he only consented to return when the government adopted a stronger line. But the really influential paper was still *The Times* under John Thaddeus Delane with its massive circulation by contemporary standards of 40,000. Relations between Delane and Aberdeen were cordial and the paper had supported his foreign policy in the 1840s. Delane was inclined to continue to do so in 1852 and during the early stages of the Eastern crisis the paper had taken a generally pro-Aberdeen line and had tried to exercise a calming influence but it gradually moved towards a more bellicose position. Kingsley Martin is probably correct in his analysis that, although *The Times* enjoyed considerable immunity from popular pressure simply because it had no rival in sight, 'ultimately *The Times* depended on the public'. There came a point beyond which Delane could not resist the groundswell of opinion.[6]

This was manifesting itself not only in the press, but still more in pamphlets and broadsheets and in the extraordinary rumours that circulated in the winter of 1853–4, which culminated in the story that Prince Albert had been committed to the Tower as a traitor in the service of Russia (or perhaps Austria – versions varied). Palmerston's resignation in December was now explained as part of a Court intrigue. Palmerston did not rush to deny this – he had a good few scores to pay off with the Court – and he undoubtedly used the press to get public backing for his policy on the Eastern question. Once war had broken out public fury turned outwards, against the Tsar. Clarendon described opinion as 'running breast-high against Nicholas'. Only when it became clear that the war was not going well was the search resumed for scapegoats and traitors at home.

The British army had been hopelessly neglected since the Napoleonic wars, despite the pleas of the Duke of Wellington for reform. The disorganization extended from the top to the bottom. Soon after the Crimean war began, Lord John Russell suggested that the War Office should be divided from the Colonial Office; the Duke of Newcastle should retain the Colonial Office and Palmerston become the Secretary of State for War. Sir George Grey could replace Palmerston at the Home Office. The suggestion was in itself a sensible one. Palmerston had long experience

of the War Office and he was, arguably, the only man in the coalition with
both the knowledge and the energy to make fundamental changes quickly.
Unfortunately, it found little favour with Aberdeen and his fellow Peelites.
Russell's motives for making the suggestion were suspect. He was
intriguing openly for the premiership and the proposal was only one of a
number of contradictory ideas he was floating at the time.

But there was another reason, too, from Aberdeen's point of view for
keeping Palmerston away from the direction of the war. Palmerston
seemed to be extending the objectives of the war far beyond the original
aim of keeping the Russians out of Constantinople. He had written to
Clarendon in March 1854 outlining the possible gains of such a successful
war against Russia. In the Baltic, Finland, taken by Russia at the end of the
Napoleonic wars, could be restored to Sweden; Poland could be re-
established in its ancient limits as an independent kingdom; the mouth of
the Danube restored to Turkey, or perhaps given to Austria; the Russian
Black Sea fleet and its base, Sebastopol, destroyed; the Crimea itself,
annexed by Catherine the Great, given back to Turkey; and finally, Russia
could be deprived of Circassia and Georgia. Aberdeen replied in horror
that these were terms that could only be dictated at the gates of Moscow
(and he, unlike Palmerston, had seen Napoleon's army after the Russian
Campaign).[7]

Palmerston, however, believed that the Cabinet in general favoured the
restoration of Poland as a war aim. Clarendon wrote in June that,
although the war had begun as a purely defensive one, 'the character of the
war is changed, and we are fighting for a state of things which will render
peace durable'. They must look afresh at all former treaties. In October
Prince Albert, usually well-informed, was convinced that Palmerston had
plans for Italy too and was manipulating the war for his own favourite
projects of 'depriving Austria of her Italian possessions & restoring
Poland'.[8] Since their ally in the war, Napoleon III, was necessarily and
publicly committed to a revisionist position and the undoing of at least part
of the Treaty of Vienna, Palmerston seemed to be raising the spectre of a
general and prolonged war to redraw the boundaries of Europe.

But such grandiose plans, if indeed Palmerston ever seriously
entertained them, began to look ridiculous in the face of the ill-success of
the British and French forces. The expedition to the Baltic, under Admiral
Napier, had some measure of success in knocking out the Russian naval
base at Bomarsund but it failed to secure any position from which an attack
upon St Petersburg itself would have become realistic. From the beginning
it had been agreed that the main theatre of operations would be the Black

Sea. The original intention had been to support the Turks in regaining the Principalities of Moldavia and Wallachia but that option was ruled out when the Russians voluntarily withdrew, leaving the Principalities under the care of neutral Austria.

The proposal that they should instead concentrate their attack upon Sebastopol was Palmerston's. The series of memoranda in the Broadlands Papers, docketed by Palmerston himself, 'Memoranda of Cabinet Ministers on my memorandum as to measures to be adopted against Russia' leave no doubt about the sequence of events.[9] Some preliminary conversations took place between some (unnamed) ministers at the home of Sir Charles Wood, the President of the Board of Control, on the evening of Wednesday 14 June. The following day Palmerston drew up and circulated a memorandum. Having entered the war they would, he said, 'lose caste in the world' if they concluded it with 'small Result'. It would be quite inadequate if the only result were the evacuation of the Principalities, which would give them no security for the future. Instead they must strike a 'heavy Blow' at the naval power and 'Territorial Divisions' of Russia. They could strike in Georgia, Circassia or the Crimea but the first two should be left to the Turks.

This memorandum was written before Palmerston knew that the Russians were pulling out of the Principalities but, in any case, he was lukewarm about campaigning there. He admitted that they were partly pledged to help Omer Pasha raise the siege of Silistria and 'If that can be accomplished early enough to leave Time for operations afterwards in the Crimea, well & good' but in no case should British and French troops cross the Danube '& entrench themselves in the unhealthy Plains of Wallachia'. It was in the Crimea that a decisive battle could be fought. At present the Russians had only 40,000 troops there. If 25,000 English and 30,000 French troops could be landed in the large Bay to the north of Sebastopol they could take the fort on the hill on the north side of the harbour and command the town and the harbour. They could also take Anapa and Poti (on the eastern shore of the Black Sea and acquired by Russia in 1829) but that was not so important. They should not put off action until next year because it would give the Russians a chance to strengthen their defences and increase their garrison. At the moment the British and French forces were 'fresh, Eager and ready for enterprize'. If they had to remain inactive until next year, their health might deteriorate. There might be political complications too. The good understanding with France might give way to suspicion. Public opinion which now supported the war might change. They should therefore suggest an early attack on Sebastopol to the French.

He added that he did not think that they were likely to accomplish much in the Baltic.

All his colleagues accepted these arguments with more, or less, enthusiasm. Granville and George Grey voiced the apparently sensible reservation (although it had disastrous consequences) that, since no one in London had enough information to make a decision on a 'professional question', the final decision must be left to Lord Raglan and the commanders in the field. Newcastle, the Secretary of State for War, with the fullest information, was the most cautious. The allied armies might not be ready to attack Sebastopol that year. He feared the French were even less prepared than the British. He agreed that the Crimea must be attacked as soon as possible 'but I would sooner postpone the attempt to a second Campaign than run the risk of a great disaster consequent upon undertaking so great an operation with insufficient means'. By contrast the Duke of Argyll, with the optimism of youth, was enthusiastic for an attack on the Crimea which would settle the war 'at once'.

The Prime Minister, Aberdeen, summed up the situation in an undated memorandum of his own. There was, he said, little disagreement among the members of the Cabinet. The destruction of Sebastopol and of the Russian fleet should be their objective and this should be attempted as soon as possible. He agreed, although he would not have done so if the siege of Silistria had not already been raised and Omer Pasha still required support on the Danube. (The siege of Silistria was raised on 23 June). He also agreed that they must leave a great deal to Raglan's discretion. The final decision was taken at a Cabinet dinner at Lord John Russell's home at Pembroke Lodge on 29 June.[10]

Premature reports reached London late in September 1854 that Sebastopol had fallen. The keenness of the disappointment when it was realized that this was not true seems to have been the immediate trigger for the change of public mood from bellicosity and confidence to anger and determination to find the culprits. The Allies had landed in the Crimea on 14 September and defeated the Russians at the battle of Alma on 20 September but the commanders, Lord Raglan and Marshal St Arnaud, had not followed up their advantage quickly enough. The Russians had been able to bring in reinforcements and complete the defences of Sebastopol.

Misfortune now followed misfortune. An attempt to reduce Sebastopol by bombardment from the sea was bungled. The allied supply fleet was destroyed in a great gale in November. The Crimean winter was unusually severe in 1854–5. The Anglo-French forces had won (on balance) the set-piece battles of Balaclava and Inkerman, in which they engaged in the autumn of 1854, but the casualties mounted, not from battle but from disease. Cholera had been prevalent in southern Europe in the summer of 1854 and it reached the British army in the Crimea in 1855. Dysentery had already taken its toll and now mortality rates in some units approached sixty per cent. Of the 18,000 British casualties in the Crimea, less than 2,000 were actually killed in battle. The rest died from disease or from wounds, many of which, given proper medical services, need not have been fatal. The proportion was probably not very different from that experienced in the Napoleonic wars but there was one very big difference – publicity.

The Crimean war was the first war fully covered in the press. William Howard Russell's famous despatches to *The Times* horrified and revolted the British public, much as the television coverage turned the American public against the Vietnam war. For the first time the public at home began to have some understanding of what war really entailed. The war had its heroes – and heroines. Florence Nightingale persuaded a reluctant War Office to let her go out to emulate the work of the French nursing orders among the wounded. Palmerston, a family friend, backed her.

But, mainly, the public was angry. In January John Arthur Roebuck, the member for Sheffield, proposed his motion in the Commons for a parliamentary inquiry into the conduct of the war. Roebuck himself probably saw this as a prelude to a radical re-organization of the army, but most of those who supported him were concerned only with the immediate crisis in the Crimea. The Cabinet was divided as to how to meet his challenge. Some, including the Prime Minister, held that what Roebuck was proposing was unconstitutional. It was Lord John Russell who, in Sir James Graham's angry words, not only ran away from the castle under siege, but left the postern gate open as he went.[11] Russell resigned, giving as part of his reason the fact that his renewed suggestion that Palmerston should become Secretary of State for War had been rejected, and even voted for Roebuck's motion. On the contrary Palmerston, in the eyes of the rest of the Cabinet, behaved very honourably in this crisis. He refused to succeed Newcastle at the War Office in circumstances where Newcastle's resignation could only be taken as an admission of responsibility for all that had gone wrong, and he led the government's defence against Roebuck's motion in the Commons.

In spite of that, Roebuck's motion was carried by 305 votes to 148, a larger majority than had been expected. Paradoxically, the House was voting for Palmerston. The pressure for his succession was increasing in the press. The Queen tried to avoid entrusting the government to him. She sent first for Lord Derby, the constitutionally correct course. He invited Palmerston to become Leader of the House of Commons and Secretary of State for War in a new coalition, but Palmerston stipulated conditions about his fellow-Whigs, which he must have known made the juncture virtually impossible. The Queen next sent for Lansdowne, who protested that he was too old, and then for Russell, who would have been delighted to have formed a government but who could find no one to join him after his recent 'treachery', as Argyll bluntly described it. Victoria now had no alternative but to send for Palmerston. He had become, as he told his brother, 'l'inévitable'.[12]

Even so, he did not find it easy to form a government. He still needed the Peelites. Aberdeen persuaded Graham, Gladstone, Argyll and Sidney Herbert to resume office. Palmerston hoped that Roebuck's motion (about the constitutionality of which he too had grave reservations) would be withdrawn once the House had a Prime Minister it felt it could trust. This time he over-rated his powers. The House insisted on the Committee. Palmerston gave in, although it cost him the resignation of Graham, Gladstone and Herbert.

Ironically, the campaign in the Crimea did not go much better after the change of government than before. It was not until September 1855 that Sebastopol finally fell. The Russians had pursued the war with less conviction after the death of Tsar Nicholas in March 1855 and the end was brought about, as Aberdeen had always believed it would be, more by international negotiation than by military action.

The Peace Conference was held in Paris, to the great gratification of Napoleon III, to whom it signified that Paris was once again the diplomatic capital of Europe. It should be remembered that in the eyes of most of Europe France, not Britain, had been the dominant partner in the war and certainly the French army had fought more efficiently, although not more bravely, than the British.

Palmerston could, and did, present the Treaty of Paris of March 1856 to the British people as a great triumph. It did check the Russians in the Near East. Sebastopol had fallen and they were compelled to agree to the neutralization of the Black Sea, which meant the disbandment of the Russian Black Sea fleet. Palmerston would have liked harder terms. He still hankered after returning the Crimea to Turkey and restoring independence to Circassia. Ironically, he had dropped any demands on behalf of Poland, although Napoleon III would have been inclined to have supported him there, mainly because he did not wish to offend Austria. The only territory which Russia was required to cede was part of

Bessarabia, which she had acquired in 1829. Turkey was formally admitted to the Concert of Europe and the Sultan made empty promises to improve the condition of the Christians within the Ottoman empire. Almost casually, Palmerston surrendered those very maritime rights – mainly to intercept neutral vessels in time of war – which Britain had maintained so fiercely during the Napoleonic wars and over which she had fought the United States in 1812. Probably it would have been impossible to have continued to have maintained most of them in the changed conditions of the late-nineteenth century but the British public was not greatly impressed by the treaty as a whole. It was criticized in the Commons and, when the heralds formally proclaimed the peace terms in the City of London, they were hissed.

The years immediately after the Crimean war suggest that the excitement which had contributed so much to the war had by no means subsided. The British public had built its hopes very high and they had been disappointed. Almost immediately, Britain plunged into two more wars, one with Persia, the other with China. In March 1857 Disraeli sarcastically challenged Palmerston to go to the country on the slogan, 'No Reform! New Taxes! Canton Blazing! Persia Invaded!'[13] The war with Persia is much less well-known than the war with China. It arose almost as an appendage to the Crimean war itself. Russia had been assiduously cultivating good relations with Persia, who had historic border quarrels with Turkey. The Russians failed to persuade the Persians to join them during the Crimean war but the British government reacted very nervously when the Persians occupied the strategic town of Herat, at that time under Afghan control. Although the Crimean war itself was only peripherally concerned with the security of India, any threat in Central Asia was taken very seriously. The British despatched a force to Bushire on the Persian Gulf and compelled the Persians to withdraw from Herat.

The comparative ill-success of British arms in the Crimea had been noted in India. The expedition to Bushire further denuded India of troops. In May 1857 the mutiny of the Bengal army began at Meerut, north of Delhi. Within a few months it had engulfed most of Bengal and a few neighbouring regions, although it never spread to the other Presidencies of Madras and Bombay. Contemporaries regarded it as simply an army mutiny. Later historians have argued as to how far it represented the first stirrings of Indian nationalism or, alternatively, the xenophobic reactions of old India which had been disturbed by the presence of Westerners. If it had succeeded it would have dealt a devastating blow, not only to Britain's economic interests in India, but also to her international prestige.

Palmerston exerted himself to ensure that troops reinforcements were sent to the Governor-General, Lord Canning, the son of Palmerston's old mentor, George Canning. Otherwise his attitude puzzled contemporaries. The Prince accused him of 'juvenile levity' and the Queen charged him with incompetence. Their complaints were echoed in parliament and in the press. Palmerston refused all offers of foreign help, whether of Belgian or Prussian troops, or Napoleon's suggestion that the reinforcements should travel by train to Marseilles to cut the journey time.[14] Palmerston's attitude may have been more calculated than his colleagues realized. Britain was dangerously exposed. Russia was still smarting from the Crimean war. France was an unpredictable friend. In addition an obscure but serious quarrel had just arisen with the United States about the Mosquito coast. Britain claimed a long-standing protectorate arrangement with the Mosquito Indians on the coast of Nicaragua. The Americans resented it as a breach of the Monroe doctrine and because it perpetuated a British presence in a very sensitive strategic area. In 1856 an American adventurer, William Walker, who had taken a prominent part in civil strife in Nicaragua, seized Greytown on the Mosquito Coast. Anglo-American relations had been strained during the Crimean war and the British government feared that the United States government might give Walker their official support. Palmerston himself favoured sending a naval force and blockading Greytown but Clarendon persuaded him to hold off blockading until the situation became clearer. In the event the American government did not support Walker. But the fact remained that in 1856–7 Britain had been very dangerously over-extended. Palmerston was always a master of bluff and his apparent insouciance and conviction that Britain could suppress the Indian Mutiny without any great exertion may well have been as effective a smoke-screen as any.

A more serious charge, although one which occurs to the twentieth-century rather than the nineteenth-century observer, was that he made no effort to enquire into the underlying forces which had generated the 'Mutiny' – apart from the attempt by the British government in India to discover whether it had all been the result of a conspiracy. In the early stages he offered Canning little public or private support for his carefully calculated policy of 'clemency'. On the contrary, he seemed disposed to side with the more extreme demands for vengeance against any who had been even peripherally associated with the rising but, characteristically, when Canning became the target of popular abuse in Britain, Palmerston rallied to the support of his subordinate.

In general, Palmerston showed neither particular interest nor particular understanding of Britain's great dependency. In December 1857 he announced that he intended to abolish the East India Company's Charter. The dual system of Crown and Company government, which had existed in India since Pitt's India Act of 1784, was undeniably cumbersome and fundamental changes had been discussed at the time of the last renewal of the Charter in 1853 during the Coalition government. The ground was not, therefore, totally unprepared; but, in the event, Palmerston's unexpected defeat in February 1858 left the short-lived Derby-Disraeli ministry to clear up the aftermath of the Mutiny and reorganize the government of India under the British Crown.

To Palmerston's irritation, in the early days of the Mutiny, Canning had intercepted some troops on their way to China to hold the line until other reinforcements arrived. This new war with China rallied all Palmerston's parliamentary opponents against him. It sprang from an apparently trivial incident, the so-called *Arrow* affair, but it lasted (with one break) until 1860, came to involve several major Powers, and marked a very important step in the forcible 'opening up' of China by the West.

It began in October 1856 when a Chinese official, Commissioner Yeh, arrested the crew of the small sailing ship, the *Arrow,* at Canton on suspicion of piracy. They claimed immunity from his jurisdiction on the grounds that the ship was registered in Hong Kong and flying the British flag. Their registration had probably expired but the mere claim was dynamite. Many Chinese resented the opening of the 'treaty ports' to foreigners and ships sailing between Hong Kong and Canton were frequently molested. In 1855 the Chinese authorities had done a deal with the British (and Americans) allowing the Westerners to extend their protection to ships sailing between the two ports. The system was supposed to be closely regulated but it had been widely abused. Ships legally flying the British flag had flagrantly engaged in smuggling and even piracy, and other ships had hoisted the British flag with no authority at all. Palmerston's reaction was rather different from that of 1840 when he protested to the Americans that 'a piece of bunting' should be no protection, although in fairness to Palmerston it must be said that the matter had passed far beyond the original incident before he heard of it.

The local British authorities over-reacted. Commissioner Yeh handed the crewmen of the *Arrow* over to Harry Parkes, the British Consul at Canton, but refused to give the guarantees Parkes demanded for the future. Sir John Bowring, the Governor of Hong Kong, ordered the navy to bombard Canton. Yeh then put a price of thirty dollars upon the head of every Englishman found in Canton and British commercial stations and ships were attacked. The British Cabinet learnt of these events in February 1857. Most of them were very uneasy and the clear opinion of the Law Officers was that Bowring had acted quite illegally, but the majority of the Cabinet was prepared to follow Palmerston's lead in believing that it would be fatal for British prestige in the 'uncivilized world' to back down. They resolved to send out a force to support Bowring.

Napoleon III was only too glad to hear of the British move. In February 1856 a French Catholic priest had been executed in Kwangsi. A French force joined the British and Canton was occupied in December 1857. Such an opportunity could not be passed up by America and Russia. In February 1858 they joined Britain and France in demanding new treaty concessions from the Chinese. In the course of the 'negotiations', the four Powers occupied the Taku forts at the mouth of the Peiko River and advanced to Tientsin on the way to the Chinese capital of Peking. The treaties of Tientsin of June 1858 not only opened up more treaty ports and placed missionary activity under official protection, but also established western-style diplomatic relations at Peking and allowed foreigners to travel to the interior. Hostilities were renewed in 1859 when the Chinese objected to the British representative, Sir Frederick Bruce, coming to Peking in a warship for the ratification ceremony. (Bruce's intransigence on the point was not entirely unjustified. The Chinese had taken advantage of the American envoy's ignorance of oriental etiquette to treat him with studied discourtesy). Worse was to follow. After the Allies had again stormed the Taku forts, the Chinese seized a number of British and French hostages, twenty of whom died. In retaliation, the British plenipotentiary, Lord Elgin, ordered the burning of the Emperor's summer palace at Peking where the hostages had been imprisoned. The Chinese agreed to some extension of the Tientsin Treaties in the new Convention of Peking. The destabilization of the Chinese empire was already manifesting itself in the outbreak of the Tai-ping rebellion.

Palmerston had not been in office during the whole of this period but he had initiated the forward movement. He had been challenged in Parliament in February and March 1857. Cobden proposed a motion of censure and Palmerston found himself facing a remarkable coalition for Cobden was supported not only by Gladstone but also by Lord John Russell, Disraeli, and Lord Robert Cecil, the future Marquess of Salisbury. Palmerston tried to repeat his triumph of the Don Pacifico debate. He deliberately avoided most of the real issues at stake and concentrated on the government's over-riding duty to protect British subjects in all circumstances. He concentrated his fire on Richard Cobden, whom he must by now have recognized as the most formidable opponent of his brand of foreign policy. Cobden had appealed to British interests, as much as to morality. Such gunboat diplomacy would have the very opposite effect to the one which Palmerston presumably intended – furthering British commerce. Palmerston in reply accused Cobden of lack of patriotism, of believing that 'everything that was English was wrong, and everything that was hostile to England was right'.[15] But he had miscalculated so far as parliamentary opinion was concerned. He did not repeat his Don Pacifico victory and lost the motion by 247 votes to 263.

Disraeli had challenged him to go to the country on his record and Palmerston accepted the challenge. The popular reaction proved to be very different from that of the parliamentarians. The public still seemed to be caught up in the jingoism which had led them to clamour for the Crimean war and to have convinced themselves that Palmerston was a great war leader (despite any disappointment with the Treaty of Paris itself) and that British subjects and the British flag must be defended in all circumstances against the 'barbarians'. Palmerston carefully avoided any reference in the election campaign to domestic issues and fought on his record in China. In his address to his own constituents in Tiverton, he assured them that he had dealt with 'an insolent barbarian wielding power at Canton, who had violated the British flag'. The strategy worked: Palmerston's enemies were almost annihilated. Cobden and Bright lost their seats in Huddersfield and Manchester; Roebuck and Lord John Russell only just retained theirs in Sheffield and the City of London. Palmerston's support ran across all classes and interests. He emerged with a clear majority of 85 in the Commons. The uncertainties of the previous ten years seemed to be at an end and Palmerston himself had won an almost unprecedented personal triumph. It was not merely a one-issue but a one-man election. As Lord Shaftesbury put it in his diary, there was only one question, 'Were you, or were you not? are you, or are you not, for Palmerston?'[16]

But Palmerston could not control the monster he had created. Barely a year later, he was out of office, for offending patriotic sentiment. In January 1858 a disillusioned Italian nationalist, Felice Orsini, threw a bomb at Napoleon III. Napoleon was unhurt but a number of bystanders were killed. It was discovered that Orsini had contacts in London and that the explosive for the bomb had come from England. Since the attempted assassination of the Austrian emperor in 1853 the British government had been under pressure from other European Powers to clamp down on what today would be called terrorist activity. The government had usually replied that British law was entirely adequate to deal with criminal conspiracies and that they had no intention of diminishing Britain's proud reputation as an asylum for political refugees – although Palmerston himself seems to have wavered at the time of the Kossuth excitement in 1853. In 1858 he decided that the time had come to act. He introduced a measure, the Conspiracy to Murder Bill, to tighten up the law.

On 19 February a radical, Milner Gibson, proposed an amendment, in effect deploring that Palmerston had given in to French pressure to the detriment of British liberties. It was seconded by John Bright who, after losing his Manchester seat, had secured election at Birmingham. Russell, Gladstone and Graham joined in the attack. Palmerston, uncharacteristically, lost his temper and with it his control of the House. With the defection of the Radicals and of substantial numbers of Whigs and Peelites, Palmerston's apparently impregnable majority had melted away. The Conservatives were believed to have indicated in advance that they would support the measure but Disraeli, supposedly on a signal from Derby in the gallery, led them into the division lobby with the Radicals. The government was defeated by 19 votes. Even more disconcertingly, the public seemed to have turned against Palmerston. The next day he was booed as he rode in Hyde Park.

Palmerston resigned. Despite occasional bad attacks of gout, which sometimes left him walking with crutches, he was still remarkably vigorous but he was nearly seventy-four and it seemed unlikely that he would ever return to office. On the other hand, although Derby had succeeded this time in forming a government, he had no majority in the Commons. No one supposed that the unholy coalition of Conservatives and Radicals which had overthrown Palmerston would last very long, since they were at odds on most domestic and foreign issues.

9

Last Ministry

Although it was unlikely that Lord Derby's precarious government would hold together indefinitely, the principal obstacle to the reconstitution of a Liberal ministry seemed to be the antagonism between Palmerston and Russell. The decisive moment came in the summer of 1859. In March Russell had introduced a motion into the Commons to reduce the £10 property qualification in the boroughs. Whigs, Liberals and Radicals of all shades of opinion voted with Russell. Even Palmerston himself felt able to do so, despite his stand against the £6 franchise in 1853, because Russell had named no specific figure to replace the £10 franchise. The motion was carried by 330 votes to 291. Derby decided to go to the country.

Derby had rightly calculated that his opponents would do less well now than they had done in the rather extraordinary general election of 1857 but the 1859 election still left the Conservatives in a minority of about 50. The opposition, however, was divided into the Palmerstonian Whigs, Lord John Russell's Whigs, the Cobdenites, some miscellaneous Radicals, the Peelites and the Irish. Derby, knowing Palmerston's views on parliamentary reform, did not think that all was lost. He invited him to join his ministry and hints were even dropped that Palmerston might be the next Conservative Prime Minister. But another issue had come between Palmerston and Derby – Italy. Palmerston preferred to make common cause with Russell after all.

The great reconciliation came at Willis's Rooms (ironically, the old Almack Club which Palmerston had frequented in his youth) on 6 June. Most of the Irish MPs had not yet arrived but the 247 newly returned members, who could reasonably call themselves Liberals, were present. Palmerston mounted the platform to general cheers, which were redoubled when he helped up the diminutive Lord John Russell. Even more remarkably, they were joined by John Bright. In fact, most issues had been settled in advance. Palmerston and Russell had met on 20 May and Palmerston had apparently withdrawn his opposition to 'a moderate measure' of parliamentary reform. They had also agreed that, immediately Parliament reassembled, Derby should be challenged with the same motion that had been carried against Melbourne in 1841 – a straight no confidence motion – and that they would co-operate in the formation of a broad-based government.

One vital question had not been settled. Should the new government be headed by Palmerston or by Russell? The question was still unresolved at the meeting of 6 June, although each man publicly offered to serve under the other. Only three Radicals – of whom the most important was Roebuck – spoke against the new-found cordiality, and they were badly received by the majority.

The meeting at Willis's Rooms is often regarded as marking the birth of the Liberal Party but it was a reconciliation rather than a completely new beginning. It re-affirmed that crucial coming together of Whigs, Peelites and even Radicals which had made up the Aberdeen Coalition of December 1852. This became apparent to contemporaries over the next few weeks. On 11 June the opposition duly carried their motion of censure and Derby resigned. The Queen tried to avoid accepting either Palmerston or Russell. Pleading that it would be invidious to try to choose between two former Prime Ministers, she sent for 'Pussy' Granville as the head of the Liberal Party in the Lords. Neither Russell nor Palmerston refused to serve under Granville but both made conditions that they must have known would be impossible to fulfil. The Queen then sent for Palmerston. She objected to him less than to Russell and probably knew that opinion in the parliamentary party was swinging in his favour.

Palmerston set about forming his Cabinet. He invited Cobden to join it but Cobden refused unless Bright was brought in too, and the views Bright had expressed during the election campaign were too 'advanced', especially on parliamentary reform, to be acceptable to the Queen, or indeed to the majority of the Cabinet. The Radicals did, however, come in – Milner Gibson at the Board of Trade and Charles Villiers (no less a radical for being Lord Clarendon's brother) at the Poor Law Board. Russell insisted on taking the Foreign Office, which effectively kept Lord Clarendon himself out of the ministry to Palmerston's regret. There were seven Whigs in the Cabinet apart from Russell himself – Lord Granville, Sir George Cornewall Lewis, Sir Charles Wood, the Duke of Somerset, Lord Elgin, Sir George Grey and the aged Lord Campbell as Lord

Chancellor – but there were also five Peelites, the Duke of Newcastle, Sidney Herbert, William Gladstone, the Duke of Argyll and Edward Cardwell. This close resemblance to the 1852 Coalition was immediately noted by Greville. He wrote on 26 June, 'This Government in its composition is curiously (and may prove fatally) like that which Aberdeen formed in 1852 of a very Peelite complexion'.[1]

In some ways Palmerston's last administration proved very unlike the 1852 Coalition. Aberdeen's government had immediately plunged into reforming legislation and would have carried much more but for the Crimean war. Palmerston, although he had contributed substantially to the earlier reforms, saw no reason to continue them. ' "Oh" ', he told G.J. Goschen in January 1864 'rubbing his hands with an air of comfortable satisfaction "there is really nothing to be done. We cannot go on adding to the Statute Book *ad infinitum*".' An incredulous Goschen added the comment, 'Be it remembered that this was in 1864. There were looming on the horizon some of the greatest problems which have ever been submitted to Parliament – Parliamentary reform, the ballot, education . . .' The most Palmerston would contemplate was 'a little law reform, or bankruptcy reform'.[2]

Almost the only significant Act passed by his first administration had been the Matrimonial Causes Act of 1857 which made it possible for people, in certain circumstances, to obtain a divorce through the courts and not, as previously, by the prohibitively expensive device of an Act of Parliament, which effectively confined divorce to the very wealthy. Gladstone had grimly opposed the measure and the two men had faced each other out in late night sittings in the hot summer of 1857. Gladstone had wilted first and the measure had passed.

The reconciliation between Palmerston and Gladstone in 1859 had been even more surprising than that between Palmerston and Russell.[3] Gladstone had been very near to rejoining the Conservatives and had even voted with the government on Russell's motion in March 1859. He had, however, gone on a mission to the Ionian Islands for Derby in 1858 and his journey back through Italy had reinforced all his earlier sympathy with Italian nationalism. On this one point he had moved very close to Palmerston on foreign policy but they were still divided on domestic questions.

The first clash came over the Budget which Gladstone as Chancellor of the Exchequer introduced in 1860. In 1853 Gladstone had promised that income tax – still regarded as an oppressive 'emergency' measure – should be abolished by 1860, by which time he expected his fiscal reforms to have worked; but the Crimean war had aborted his reform programme. He now saw no chance of abolishing the tax and instead proposed to raise it from 9*d.* to 10*d.* in the pound to pay for another radical reform, the abolition of the Paper Duties, the tax on books and newspapers. This was particularly hated because, earlier in the century, it had been manipulated to try to prevent the spread of seditious reading and it was still, reviled as a 'tax on knowledge'. Gladstone forced the proposal through the Cabinet in the face of the Prime Minister's opposition.

Although the suspicion that Palmerston deliberately intrigued with Derby seems unfounded,[4] his attitude encouraged the Lords to reject the measure, although the constitutional propriety of their rejecting a finance measure passed by the Commons was already open to question. A major clash between the two houses seemed imminent. Gladstone and the Radicals wanted to send the Bill back to the Lords. Palmerston tried to defuse the situation by referring the matter to the Committee of Privileges but the Committee reported against the Lords. The following year Gladstone insisted on including the abolition of the Paper Duties among his proposals and, what was more, insisted on including all his measures in a single Finance Bill. The repercussions of the Upper House rejecting the whole Budget were more than the Lords cared to risk, and the Paper Duties were duly abolished.

Palmerston repeatedly lost his temper with Gladstone but his relations with Lord John Russell were remarkably harmonious – so much so that they became sardonically nicknamed 'Robin Hood' and 'Little John'. This was the more surprising in that Palmerston successfully blocked all attempts at parliamentary reform. In the discussions of 1857–8 he had moved some way to accepting the so-called 'fancy franchises', the proposal that members of the learned professions, those earning certain salaries or having certain stipulated savings, for example, should be eligible to vote. A rather vague promise of further reforms was included in the party's election campaign of 1859 and Russell did introduce a Bill into the Commons in 1860 but it was ill-received by both right and left and in June it was withdrawn. Palmerston had never lost his fear of the hold he believed that the trade unions would have over the working classes, who would not be free agents. He was particularly horrified when Gladstone, influenced by the staunchness of the Lancashire cotton operatives during the American Civil War, said in May 1864 that he did not see why every man, who was not mentally incapacitated, should not have the vote. This espousal, at least in principle, of universal suffrage was more than Palmerston could bear from a man who had previously been a fellow-opponent of reform. He commented sarcastically, 'If every sane Man has the right why does it not belong to every sane woman who is equally affected by Legislation and Taxation.' He thought that even Gladstone would see the absurdity of that. Palmerston based his opposition to parliamentary reform on the old grounds that 'the vote is not a *Right* but a *Trust*.'[5] It must be exercised publicly on behalf of the community. It followed that the secret ballot was unthinkable — although that, of course, would have allayed most of Palmerston's fears about the working man being pressurized by both his employer and his union. In the end the reformers, even John Bright, seem to have given up and waited for Palmerston to die or retire. He was, after all, approaching eighty.

Palmerston was equally reactionary on most social issues. Perhaps it was to some extent the simple effect of old age. As Home Secretary he had been enlightened, if firm, in his attitude to penal reform. In 1862 he gave in to panic about a wave of mugging (garrotting) in London. He urged the Home Secretary to introduce flogging for robbers and to abolish the ticket-of-leave system, which he himself had set up in 1853, even to the extent of recalling all those out on parole. The first, but not the second, proposal was adopted. He also opposed the abolition of public executions, which he believed had an important deterrent effect.

As an Irish landlord, he opposed any concessions towards tenants' security against eviction — 'tenant right is landlord's wrong', said Palmerston — and even any legal right to compensation for improvements made by an outgoing tenant. The 1860 Bill on the latter point was passed, despite Palmerston's disapproval, but so worded as to make successful claims difficult. Palmerston accused those who supported such measures of being communists.[6]

He disliked the introduction of any form of competitive examination for entry into the civil service. He made the point that ability to pass examinations was no guarantee of official talents — although he had no answer to Trevelyan's argument that what you were testing was the candidate's ability to perform the tasks expected of him, and that the only tasks which had usually been demanded of students was to become proficient in classics and mathematics.

Shaftesbury's influence was sufficiently strong to ensure that Palmerston still felt some sympathy for factory reform and improvements in working-class housing. Shaftesbury's influence was also felt in another field, that of ecclesiastical appointments. Palmerston himself had no strong religious convictions but he distrusted the Tractarian (or Oxford) movement, partly because it was stirring up what he saw as totally unnecessary dissensions in the Church of England, partly because, like many Englishmen of the time, he regarded it as a Trojan horse for the advancement of Roman Catholicism. He was happy to accept the advice of his evangelical son-in-law, and Shaftesbury was delighted to recommend a succession of Low Church candidates, who became known to their disgusted opponents as the 'Shaftesbury Bishops'.[7]

Generally by this time, Palmerston seems to have come to dislike any kind of change in the system which was familiar to him. No one could deny his conservatism at home, yet in his conduct of foreign affairs he was still credited with a good deal of liberalism. Was this correct? The Italian question had erupted in time to play a part in the 1859 election. Without it, Gladstone would probably not have joined Palmerston.

In July 1859 Napoleon III and Cavour, the Prime Minister of Piedmont-Sardinia, had reached a secret agreement at Plombières that France would help to expel the Austrians from northern Italy, in return for the cession of Savoy and Nice. The Austrians were provoked into issuing an ultimatum to the Piedmontese in April 1859. When the ultimatum was rejected, the Austrian army crossed the River Ticino into Piedmont and Napoleon came to his ally's aid. In Britain the Court and the Derby administration, which was still in power, were sympathetic to Austria and alarmed by French aggression. At first the only question seemed to be whether Britain would remain neutral or actively aid Austria.

The complication was that by this time the British middle classes were strongly pro-Italian. So were Lord John Russell and Gladstone. Palmerston had always hoped to be spared this stark choice of supporting either France or Austria in Italy and it is difficult not to believe that he made unscrupulous use of the issue in the general election. He himself was returned unopposed at Tiverton but he still felt it necessary to prepare a speech for the hustings, which would be in effect an election address. He gave a copy to Borthwick in advance – he was always considerate in helping journalists to meet their deadlines – but the advance copy differed substantially from what he actually said on the hustings. The original draft was very moderate, insisting on British neutrality and protesting that the Derby government must not let Britain be drawn in on the Austrian side.

This was in line with what he had said to Granville in January when he had written,

As for myself, I am very Austrian north of the Alps, but very anti-Austrian south of the Alps. The Austrians have no business in Italy, and they are a public nuisance there . . . I should therefore rejoice and feel relieved if Italy up to the Tyrol were freed from Austrian dominion and military occupation. But in politics as in other matters, it is not enough to show a desirable end, one must always be able to point out means of arriving at it, the objectionable nature of which shall not counter-balance the advantage of the result to be accomplished. Now the Austrians cannot be driven out of their Italian provinces without a desperate struggle . . . A war begun to drive the Austrians out of Italy would infallibly succeed in its immediate object, but it might and probably would lead to other consequences much to be deplored. It is greatly for the interests of Europe that Austria should continue to be a great Power in the centre of the Continent; but if she was deeply engaged in a conflict in Italy, the Hungarians would rise, and Russia would threaten on the Galician frontier, and instead of seeing Italy freed, and nothing more, we might find Austria dismembered . . . I hope from what you say [Granville was in France] that the Emperor Napoleon will be overruled and that peace will be maintained; but if war should unfortunately break out, I am quite sure that the only course for England is neutrality. We must stand aloof. Public opinion would not allow the government to declare war against France, Sardinia and Russia, in order to maintain Austria in Italy, and of course it is out of the question that we should take part against Austria. England is a party to the treaties which give Austria her Italian provinces, and we have no pretence for violating or disregarding those treaties.[8]

This undoubtedly represented Palmerston's considered judgement but his Tiverton speech left a very different impression on the minds of the public. They heard it as a forthright condemnation of the Austrian presence in Italy and an openly expressed hope that they would be driven out. *The Times* had no difficulty in recognizing it as an election manoeuvre, although they expressed their opinion delicately. 'Lord Palmerston', said the editorial 'knew very well what England would look to find in a speech of his at this crisis'.[9]

The intervention of Napoleon III raised the most difficult and dangerous questions. Britain was already in the grip of a war scare. It had its origins not only in the very name of Bonaparte but also in the naval building programme which the French had undertaken since the Crimean war. The favourite War Office nightmare was of the 'steam bridge' which the French could throw across the Channel for long enough to land an army which could seize Britain's almost totally unprotected dockyards and arsenals. Palmerston to some extent shared the public concern. He wrote to Gladstone in December 1859, 'We should be reduced to the rank of a third-rate power, if no worse happened to us. That such a landing is, in the present state of things, possible, must be manifest.' He compelled his reluctant Chancellor of the Exchequer to disgorge nine million pounds,

mainly for the erection of new fortifications at Portsmouth, Plymouth,
Chatham and Cork. He was also energetic in re-organizing the Volunteer
movement and supplying them with rifles – although his enthusiasm was
tempered by his fear that in the manufacturing towns of the midlands and
north, they might be infiltrated by Chartists and Socialists.[10]

Anti-French feeling slowly subsided, especially after the Cobden Treaty
of 1860 began a new period of prosperous trading relations between the
two countries but, while it lasted, it added yet another complication to the
need to co-ordinate British and French policy in Italy. The MP, Monkton
Milnes, summed up very accurately what the British public would really
have liked when he told a French friend, 'We want, first, that the Austrians
should beat you French thoroughly; next, we want that the Italians should
be free; and then we want them to be very grateful to us for doing
nothing'.[11] Palmerston came very close to fulfilling the second and third
parts of this programme. Indeed, he showed some of the skills he had
shown in the 1830s in tying French hands by co-operating with them,
despite the fact that he had considerable difficulties in carrying his
colleagues with him. The Prince Consort was very alarmed about the
Italian situation and Granville regularly leaked Cabinet discussions to him.
The line up was usually Palmerston, Russell and Gladstone against the rest.
The majority would have preferred a policy of strict neutrality but the
minority hoped for some more active intervention.

Palmerston had been in office barely a month when Napoleon, appalled
by the bloodshed, concluded the armistice of Villafranca with Austria.
Piedmont was not consulted. Villafranca transferred Lombardy to
Piedmont and allowed her to acquire Parma and Piacenza but Austria
retained Venetia. Palmerston himself would have been content to see
Piedmont take Venetia. He had told Russell in June, 'I can see no danger to
English interests in the annexation of Venice to such a State; on the
contrary, a State possessing Genoa and Venice would of necessity make
commerce its vital principle, and having two seaports, both of which
might, in case of war with England, be blockaded by British squadrons,
such a State would have a double inducement against a rupture with
England.'[12] Under the Villafranca arrangements, Modena and Tuscany
were to be restored to their Dukes, who had fled, and the Romagna, which
had declared its independence, was returned to the Pope. Austria and
France agreed to support the idea of an Italian Confederation under the
Pope. The last point did not commend itself to Protestant England,
especially as the Papal forces had suppressed the rebels with considerable
cruelty in Umbria and the Marches. British opinion became even more

disapproving when, in March 1860, Napoleon claimed his reward of Savoy and Nice despite the fact that he had left Piedmont in the lurch.

In January 1860 Palmerston supported Russell in trying to push through an alliance with France to defend Italy against any further use of force by Austria but the majority of the Cabinet opposed them and Clarendon even believed that the Queen had refused to announce such a policy in the Speech from the Throne at the opening of the parliamentary session.[13] As over the Paper Duties, a major constitutional crisis could have arisen but it was averted by the suggestion from the French themselves that it would be more helpful if Britain asked both France and Austria not to interfere further in Italy. This return to a neutral stance was greeted with relief by both the Court and the majority of the Cabinet.

In the spring of 1860 Cavour was able, by using the device of a plebiscite to ascertain the wishes of the people, to add Tuscany and Emilia (Bologna, Modena, Parma and Piacenza) to Piedmont. In April a rising took place at Palermo in Sicily. The following month Garibaldi, with the secret connivance of Cavour and the King Victor Emmanuel, sailed from Genoa to Sicily with his thousand Redshirts. Palmerston suspected another bargain like Plombières and feared Napoleon had been promised Genoa and Sardinia for his acquiescence. He even considered supporting the King of Naples, a course rendered more possible by the fact that the notorious King Bomba had just died and been succeeded by the comparatively inoffensive Francis II. Garibaldi secured control of Sicily in a matter of weeks.

On 17 May Palmerston suggested to Russell that the British fleet should be sent to the Straits of Messina between Sicily and the Italian mainland. What exactly it was to do when it got there changed from day to day but Palmerston saw that it gave Britain a bargaining counter which she did not otherwise possess. In July the French Ambassador suggested that the British and French fleets should co-operate to prevent Garibaldi crossing the Straits. Palmerston, who had believed that Napoleon, the Piedmontese and Garibaldi were all in league, was surprised but initially inclined to agree. It was Russell who persuaded him that, if the Neapolitans really supported Garibaldi, Britain would lose all influence in southern Italy by such a course. Once again Palmerston opted for neutrality as, on consideration, did Napoleon. Garibaldi crossed the Straits on 19 August and was in Naples by 7 September. Thereafter the Italian drama continued without any real assistance from Palmerston. Cavour occupied the Papal States to anticipate Garibaldi. Plebiscites gave Piedmont, Naples, Sicily, Umbria and the Marches in the autumn of 1860 and the first Italian

Parliament, representing the whole country except Venetia and Rome itself, met in Turin in February 1861. The British public was satisfied. Palmerston's claim to have been an architect of Italian unity was mostly hollow but he had said the right things in public and a British fleet had been visibly on the scene.

The next great foreign policy issue, the Amercian Civil War, brought Palmerston close to disaster. Palmerston, like most upper-class men, sympathized with the Southern States. He genuinely disliked slavery (although his crusading zeal had been more directed against the slave trade than against slavery as an institution) but, at the outset, the war concerned the preservation of the Union rather than the slavery issue. Domestic politics and his own inclinations prevented President Lincoln from condemning slavery immediately and the ostensible cause of the war was the question of State, as against Federal, rights. Palmerston had the reputation of being one of the most anti-American of British politicians. What he really disliked was the brash, challenging policy of the Yankee North – at times uncomfortably like his own. The gentlemen of the South were more congenial. Moreover, it could be argued that the United States was too big and unwieldy to remain a single country and that in recent history large-scale secessions, like that of Texas from the Mexican empire, had always succeded. Finally, the British dependence on Southern cotton for her textile industry made an accommodation with the South seem more urgent than one with the North.

Early in May 1861 Britain proclaimed her neutrality between the two parties. This could in itself be regarded as offensive by the North since it implicitly recognized the Southern States as belligerents, and not mere rebels. On the other hand, the British obliged the North by recognizing the validity of their blockade of the South, although it was essentially a 'paper blockade' of the kind condemned by the Treaty of Paris of 1856.

The ambiguity of British feeling, even at the highest level, was well known in the Southern States and in the autumn of 1861 they sent two leading politicians, James M. Mason and John Slidell, to try to secure full recognition for the South in Europe. Mason and Slidell embarked on a British mail steamer, the *Trent*, at Havana. An American naval officer, Captain Wilkes, acting without orders from his government, intercepted the *Trent* and took off the two Southerners. The British Law Officers' first opinion (which they subsequently revised) was that this was not illegal. But the British public was not particularly interested in legal opinions. They had been touched in a sore spot and from Palmerston of all men they expected a strong response. Palmerston himself thought that there would be war and does not seem to have regretted it. But the Prince Consort, in his last political intervention before his death, toned down Russell's belligerent demand for satisfaction. The American Secretary of State, William Seward, returned a conciliatory reply but some ten days after Russell received this, the *Morning Post* published a strong article, believed to stem from Palmerston himself, threatening war if Mason and Slidell were not released. Troop reinforcements were sent to Canada.[14] The pressure worked: Mason and Slidell were released and reached Southampton in February 1862.

Even Lincoln's Emancipation Proclamation in the autumn of 1862, freeing all the slaves in the rebellious States, did not alter Palmerston's own attitude. When in March 1865 Mason asked him if he would recognize the Confederacy if the Confederate States themselves abolished slavery, Palmerston replied that this was not the issue. As in Italy, Palmerston was less concerned with deep questions of morality or justice than with practical politics. He became more willing to co-operate with the North, not because of their attitude on slavery but because it became apparent that they were likely to win.

Britain's neutrality was compromised on two occasions. The Confederate States were anxious to obtain ships from Britain. The British government failed to act in time to stop one such ship, the *Alabama,* sailing from Liverpool in July 1862 but they did stop two others, the so-called Laird's rams (ships fitted with ramming devices) sailing in September 1863. The legal issue was a complicated one. If the North and the South had been two ordinary belligerent Powers, there could have been no objection in international law to Britain supplying armaments to either side. But the British government was still undecided whether to treat the South as a State or as a group of rebels. The same unresolved dilemma prevented them from agreeing to Napoleon III's suggestion that Britain and France should offer their joint mediation. Palmerston himself was inclined towards recognition – although less inclined than Russell and Gladstone – but his Cabinet was divided and he decided to play for time until, in 1864–5, the military superiority of the North became clear. It was ironic that it was Gladstone who, in 1872, was called upon to pay what most British people regarded as the inflated American claims for the depredations of the *Alabama* on Northern shipping.

Palmerston's attitude to the American Civil War had been vacillating but his luck held. The balance of power in Europe was shifting and here Palmerston could not, or at least did not, play his cards with the same skill as formerly. In 1863 the Poles once again rose against the Russians. There was little the Western Powers could do to help them, especially as the Russians had successfully bargained for Prussian support for any measures they might take to suppress the rebellion. Napoleon III tried to persuade Palmerston to join him in protesting and, a little later, to agree to a summoning of a new Congress of all the Great Powers of Europe. Palmerston had been willing to co-operate with Napoleon against Russia in 1853 and in Italy in 1858–60, despite the misgivings of those of his colleagues who saw France as the main danger to the stability of Europe. His reaction was now sharply different. He seems to have suspected that Napoleon was looking for an excuse to attack Prussia on the Rhine. He certainly saw the proposal for a new Congress to revise the Vienna Settlement as totally unacceptable.

Palmerston's basic conservatism even in foreign affairs and his belief that the Vienna Settlement was still and should remain the foundation of the European order comes out very clearly in a long letter he wrote to King Leopold of the Belgians in November 1863. 'Our answer to the Emperor's proposals', he wrote 'has been, in substance, that we do not admit that the Treaties of Vienna have ceased to be in force, inasmuch as, on the contrary, they are still the basis of the existing arrangements of Europe.' Russia was not likely to give in over Poland. 'But if the Congress were to enter upon the wide field of proposed and possible changes of territory what squabbles and animosities would ensue. Russia would ask to get back all she lost by the Treaty of Paris; Italy would ask for Venetia and Rome; France would plead geography for the frontier of the Rhine; Austria would show how advantageous it would be to Turkey to transfer to Austria Bosnia or Moldo-Wallachia; Greece would have a word to say about Thessaly and Epirus; Spain would wonder how England could think of retaining Gibraltar; Denmark would say that Sleswig is geographically part of Jutland, and that, as Jutland is an integral part of Denmark, so ought Sleswig to be so too; Sweden would claim Finland; and some of the greater German states would strongly urge the expediency of mediatizing a score of the smaller Princes.'[15] Palmerston had no intention of opening such a can of worms. But Napoleon III was offended and it influenced his refusal to co-operate with Britain over the next crisis, Schleswig-Holstein.

Ironically, Palmerston's handling of the Schleswig-Holstein question had been generally regarded as his most solid success in the difficult days of 1848–9. The problem arose from the fact that the Duchies of Schleswig and Holstein were united with the Crown of Denmark, much as Britain and Hanover had once been, by a personal union although the Salic Law, which forbade succession through the female line, applied in the Duchies but not in Denmark. In 1846 the King of Denmark, Christian VIII, tried to forestall the possibility of the succession passing to different claimants by declaring the Duchies incorporated into Denmark. The considerable German population in the Duchies protested. Holstein (although not Schleswig) was part of the German Confederation and the Frankfort Parliament supported the Duchies and wished to incorporate them into the new German state. A Prussian army actually entered the Duchies. The Russians declared their support for the King of Denmark and a European war seemed possible. A conference was hastily convened in London, with Palmerston in the chair. The question was almost unbelievably complicated. Palmerston was to say in 1864 that only three people had ever understood it – the Prince Consort who was by then dead, a German professor who was now in a lunatic asylum and himself, who had forgotten all about it. Numerous compromise solutions were suggested and failed but in May 1852 the Great Powers and the Danes signed the Convention of London. By it Duke Christian of Augustenburg renounced his claim to the Duchies in favour of Christian of Glücksberg, the heir presumptive to the Danish throne. The problem seemed to be solved.

Christian VIII had died in January 1848 and had been succeeded by his son, Frederick VII, who had no male children. Trying to make the situation more secure, Frederick made several attempts, of doubtful legality under the terms of the Convention of London, to incorporate the Duchies constitutionally into Denmark. The last of these, in the spring of 1863, provoked a strong reaction, not only from the Germans in the Duchies but also from the German Diet. As it happened, British eyes were particularly directed towards Denmark at this time because Christian of Glücksberg's daughter, Alexandra, had just married the Prince of Wales. Palmerston advised Frederick VII to withdraw the new constitution but he also determined to warn off any intervention by the German Diet. In July he told the Commons that 'the independence, the integrity, and the rights of Denmark' must be maintained and he was convinced 'if any violent attempt were made to overthrow those rights and interfere with that independence, those who made the attempt would find in the result that it would not be Denmark alone with which they would have to contend.'[16] The speech was later to acquire notoriety but Gladstone noted that at the time it attracted no great attention.

The situation was further complicated in December 1863 when Frederick VII died. As Queen Victoria remarked he could not have chosen a more unfortunate moment. Frederick of Augustenberg, the son of Duke Christian, claimed the Duchies, arguing that he was not bound by his father's renunciation. The German Diet denounced the Convention of 1852 and sent troops into Holstein. The real threat came, however, from another direction and one which Palmerston seems to have been slow to recognize. Otto von Bismarck, the new Prime Minister of Prussia, was determined to secure control of the vital strategic area of Holstein, including the port of Kiel. He calculated that this could best be done, not by supporting Frederick of Augustenberg, but by persuading the Austrians to join him in a military intervention, nominally to uphold the Convention of 1852.

The Danes appealed to Britain, relying at least in part on Palmerston's speech of July 1863. Throughout the vital early months of 1864 Palmerston was frequently seriously ill with gout but, in any case, there was little he could do. Russell suggested that they should send a fleet to Copenhagen but Palmerston knew when his bluff had been called – and in rather different circumstances from those he had envisaged the previous July. Britain could not fight a land war on the continent without an ally and neither France nor Russia would support her. In any case Palmerston did not want to encourage France to cross the Rhine. He told Russell, 'The conquest of that territory [Prussia's Rhenish provinces] by France would be an evil for us, and would seriously affect the position of Holland and Belgium'. It would be unwise to send a squadron to the Baltic, unless it was clearly understood that it was a preliminary to action on land. 'On the whole', he concluded 'I should say that it would be best for us to wait awhile before taking any steps in these matters.'[17] The most he could do was to insist that the Austrians must not send a fleet.

In April a Conference met in London of all the interested parties, including the German Confederation, and an armistice was arranged but the Danes, perhaps still believing that in the last resort the British would not let them be defeated, refused to make any concession so long as the Duchies were occupied. On 25 June the British Cabinet discussed whether to send a fleet to help in the defence of Copenhagen if necessary. The proposal was carried on Palmerston's casting vote but he then conceded that it would be impossible to act with such a divided Cabinet. The war was resumed and by the Treaty of Vienna of October 1864 the Danes surrendered the Duchies into the keeping of Prussia and Austria.

Palmerston once again had to meet a major challenge in parliament. A motion was introduced into both Houses, regretting that the Ministers had failed to uphold the integrity and independence of Denmark and had thus lowered the influence of England in the councils of Europe and diminished the securities for peace. It was carried in the Lords by nine votes. It looked as if it would be carried in the Commons, where Disraeli introduced it. The debate lasted, like the Don Pacifico debate in 1850, for four nights. Palmerston won it by a mixture of vigorous oratory and clever parliamentary tactics. He accused his critics of lack of patriotism for suggesting that British influence had diminished and unashamedly claimed credit for his government's domestic record, particularly Gladstone's financial policies (most of which he had privately opposed). Finally, fearing he could not carry a direct negative of the motion he accepted A.W. Kinglake's amendment in favour of non-intervention between Denmark and Germany. The Cobdenites could hardly fail to vote for the amendment and Palmerston won by eighteen votes. His principal opponent, Disraeli, could not withhold his admiration particularly when, 'Lord P., after the division, scrambled up a wearying staircase to the ladies' gallery. My informant [unnamed] saw the ladies' gallery open, and Lady Palmerston advance, and they embraced! An interesting scene, and what pluck! To mount those dreadful stairs at three o'clock in the morning and eighty years of age!'[18]

Palmerston was to win another general election in the summer of 1865 but political success, like bodily vigour, was becoming something of an illusion. Despite the Prime Minister's reluctance, promises had to be held out about parliamentary reform. The failure to deal effectively with the Irish problem was beginning to bear dreadful fruit in the Fenian outrages. His own main interest was still in foreign affairs, and despite his ill-success over Schleswig-Holstein, one of his last letters to Russell shows remarkable prescience about the future balance of Europe. Russia, he predicted, would become a power as great as the Roman empire. She could, he thought, become mistress of all Asia, except British India, whenever she chose. A strong Prussia, and a strong Germany, would be essential to restrain Russia.[19]

His mind was clear to the end but his attacks of what were called gout but may really have been kidney failure became increasingly severe. In August 1865 he went from Broadlands to Brocket in Hertfordshire, which his wife had inherited from her brother, Lord Melbourne, apparently to be within better reach of medical advice, but he did not curtail his activities. Early in October he caught a chill and died on the 18th, two days before his eighty-first birthday. He died, as he would probably have wished, with his despatch box on his bedside table and a half-completed letter before him.

10

The Legacy

Palmerston had wished to be buried in the family vault at Romsey Abbey near Broadlands but Gladstone intervened and insisted that he ought to be buried in Westminster Abbey alongside his great predecessors, William Pitt, Lord Castlereagh and George Canning. The Queen was persuaded to decree it. By 1865 Palmerston was a public institution, much as Victoria herself was to be thirty years later. It was hard to imagine the country without him. As *The Times'* editorial said the day after his death, his passing marked the end of an epoch.

In domestic affairs, matters soon took another direction. In 1867 Disraeli, another great opportunist, persuaded parliament to pass the Second Reform Act. The beneficiary was William Gladstone, who won the 1868 election and began to implement reforms in Ireland, education and the civil service and even introduced the secret ballot; some of the measures Gladstone introduced had been held back since the early 1850s, others went far beyond anything envisaged then.

The nine years of Palmerston's premiership saw almost no advance in the field of domestic reforms. Two very different interpretations are possible of the significance of this. It can be regarded as a period of missed opportunities, perhaps the very period when Britain's slow decline began, relative to other Powers such as the United States and Germany. Britain was in the forefront of the first industrial revolution at the end of the eighteenth century. She was not in the forefront of the second a century later. Complacency, the belief that she could never be overtaken, played its part. Britain was very slow to modernize.

Palmerston certainly cannot escape all blame for this. He doughtily defended an antiquated franchise which could not adequately reflect the whole nation's interests. Despite his first-hand knowledge of Ireland, he always refused to tackle any of the underlying problems, at a time when a solution might still have been possible. He was an early convert to *laissez-faire* and free trade, liberating ideas in the time of Adam Smith, but hardening into dogma by the late-nineteenth century. It inhibited state action even where that might have been beneficial. In matters like education Britain lagged far behind her rivals.

The other explanation, more favourable to Palmerston, is that this decade provided a necessary breathing space, a time for consolidation. The strongest evidence for this is that there seemed to be no vociferous demand for further reforms, parliamentary or otherwise. This was an argument that Palmerston himself repeatedly used, although it is weakened by the outbursts of violent protest, such as the so-called 'Battle of Hyde Park', which preceded the Second Reform Act of 1867. Certainly, there were forces emerging in British life which Palmerston never understood. On one level, if John Vincent's arguments are correct, a new Liberal party was being created in the country, which only later found its parliamentary leadership in Gladstone.[1] Palmerston's reaction to the working classes, with their trade union organizations, always seems to have been one of fear and distrust. Perhaps he never quite forgot his childhood memories of the mobs he encountered in France in 1792.

The famous concluding words of Guedalla's biography, that with Palmerston's death, 'the last candle of the Eighteenth Century was out' are usually taken to refer to Palmerston's personal style and private life and it has rightly been retorted that, in those, Palmerston was not so much an eighteenth-century figure as a Regency man. But in a more profound sense they may well be true for Palmerston never deserted his own father's political principles as a Whig who believed in the finality of the Glorious Revolution of 1688. Palmerston's whole objection to the advance of the working classes was that it would destroy the balance of the constitution. He wrote to Russell in November 1853 that he objected to his reform proposals because they would upset 'the existing balance of legislative and political power as possessed by the several classes of the community and tend to take away a large portion of such power from the aristocracy, the landowners, and the gentry, and to give it over to the manufacturing, commercial, and working classes' and to Lansdowne the following month that he could not be a party to the continual 'Transfer of Representation from one Class to another' and to a proposal which would 'overpower Intelligence & Property by Ignorance & Poverty'.[2] In that Palmerston was another King Canute.

How does this fit with his foreign policy? Krein[3] in his study of

Palmerston's last ministry suggests that everything was really geared to domestic policy and the retention of power at home. *The Times* in its obituary articles in October 1865 put the matter a little more delicately. 'Lord Palmerston', it said 'was a patriot in this sense: that he had the art to find out what his country wished to do, and the will to assist it' and 'He saw in Public Opinion a force and a meaning which no statesman before him had realized . . . all through his political life Lord Palmerston bowed to this deity, recognized its power, and used it as he could'.[4]

To some extent, Canning had anticipated him in this. Temperley, in what remains one of the best analyses, makes an interesting comparison between Canning and Palmerston, 'Canning', he wrote 'is most remarkable for a profound intellectual conception of foreign policy . . . Here we have the essential difference between Canning and Palmerston. The one took no step without weighing its consequences in relation to the whole . . . the other was a man of expedients and of the moment. Both believed in public opinion, but Canning usually controlled what Palmerston sometimes had to follow.' Yet Temperley could not altogether withhold his admiration for Palmerston. 'He was,' he says 'a man of great courage and of boundless energy and vivacity . . . He was indeed not a man of principle or system, yet he was a superb opportunist. He excelled in calling "bluffs" and in making them. It was not the highest statesmanship but it often served.'[5]

There is a consistency of judgement about Palmerston from the best-informed of his contemporaries to the best-informed of modern historians, like Bourne and Temperley. Palmerston was an extremely intelligent man, as well as what today would be called a charismatic personality. He was a man of quite exceptional energy and his long years at the top gave him a commanding position. He was an instinctive politician, who usually guessed right how other men, especially politicians, would react to things – hence his ability to make and call bluffs. But he did not have what Temperley calls 'a profound intellectual conception of foreign policy' – and that had its own dangers.

Palmerston had, of course, a general framework of ideas within which he acted – a desire for peace and stability in Europe to be achieved by a balance of power, although 'balance of power' could mean different things at different times; a preference for constitutional states, partly because that usually meant a strong middle class, which made such countries good trading partners for Britain, and national prosperity too was a Palmerstonian aim; to these were added Palmerston's quite genuine impulses in favour of reforms such as the abolition of the slave trade. But his pragmatism, while giving ample room for manoeuvre, also meant that he could embark on courses without seeing clearly where they would lead.

This really began in the great unheavals of 1848–9. There was in fact very little that Britain, whose strength lay in sea power, could do to influence these momentous events. Palmerston was well aware of that. But suddenly he found that he had tapped an unexpected vein of popularity at home by speaking forcefully even when he could not act forcefully. Ironically, Palmerston had always previously been aware that one of his greatest weaknesses had been his inability to project his policies effectively in the Commons, let alone to the public. The temptation to exploit his new found powers was too great. He had already discovered the importance of using the press. The later Palmerston had the confidence to 'stump' round the country in a manner which would have seemed extraordinary to Canning, although it was to be fully exploited by Gladstone. In 1860, for example, he made a highly successful tour of Yorkshire. The working classes in Leeds were particularly enthusiastic, so much so that an angry John Bright told Cobden, 'They rush to do honour to the man who despises and insults them.'[6] Editorials in *The Times* after his death made much of his ability to get on with all sorts and conditions of men, whether on the hustings at Tiverton, at agricultural dinners or at Mechanics' Institutes, 'He attained', it said 'with the middle classes of this country a popularity such as no other statesman of our time has equalled.' The paper carried reports of public grief in many towns and cities as diverse as Edinburgh, Leeds and Southampton.[7]

But Palmerston had purchased that popularity at a price. In his latter years he had continually told the public what it wanted to hear. In doing so he had created a myth of British foreign policy, which did not even conform very closely to his actual policy. His real policy was usually cautious, intricate and carefully adjusted to what could actually be achieved. The popular image was one of Britain giving the law to the world. A little after Palmerston's death this picture of the bullying, but successful, Palmerston was to merge all too easily with new ideas of Social Darwinism and the survival of the fittest. It was to play its part in Lord Beaconsfield's handling of the Eastern question in 1876–8 and later in the aggressive foward movement of the new imperialism of the 1880s and 1890s. The myth has actually been reinforced in the twentieth century. As Britain's real power in the world has declined so some people have sought reassurances in the picture of a once-dominant Britain, led by Palmerston who was a kind of incarnation of John Bull. Even in the middle of the nineteenth century, it had little reality. It might be more truly reassuring to reassess how much Palmerston, as the Foreign Secretary and Prime Minister of one great power among five, achieved by a skilful playing of the diplomatic game.

Notes

Notes to Chapter 1

[1] *The Times,* 16 Dec., *Morning Herald* 17 Dec. 1853.
[2] B.L., Add. MSS. 43049, Palmerston to Aberdeen, 12 Feb. 1854. For discussion see below pp. 88–9.
[3] See below p. 81.
[4] Palmerston to Gladstone, 23 Aug. 1865, P. Guedalla, *Gladstone and Palmerston* (1928), p. 342.
[5] A.R.D. Elliott, *Life of George Joachim Goschen* (1911), vol 1, p. 65; see below p. 107.
[6] Palmerston to Leopold of the Belgians, 15 Nov, 1864, H.L. Bulwer and E. Ashley, *Life of Viscount Palmerston* (1871–6), vol 2, pp. 247–8.
[7] Quoted in J. Ridley, *Lord Palmerston* (1970), p. 528.
[8] For instance see below p. 47.
[9] C.K. Webster, *The Foreign Policy of Palmerston, 1830–1841* (1951), vol 1, p. v.
[10] G.B. Henderson, *Crimean War Diplomacy and other Essays* (1947), pp. 198–9.
[11] D. Southgate, *'The Most English Minister . . .': the policies and politics of Palmerston* (1966), p. xxiv.
[12] H.C.F. Bell, *Lord Palmerston* (1936), vol 2, pp. 424–9.
[13] *The Times,* 19 Oct 1865.
[14] Duke of Argyll, *Autobiography and Memoirs,* (1907), vol 1, p. 323.
[15] K. Bourne, *Palmerston: the Early Years, 1784–1841* (1982), p. 628.

Notes to Chapter 2

[1] James Hannay, 'The Family of Temple', *The Cornhill Magazine,* XII (1865), 749–60
[2] Ibid, 752.
[3] H.L. Bulwer and E. Ashley, *Life of Viscount Palmerston* (3rd edn., 1871), vol. 1, p. 5.
[4] Earl of Minto, *Life and Letters of Sir Gilbert Elliot, First Earl of Minto,* ed. Countess of Minto (1874), vol. 1, pp. 277, 311–12.

[5] P. Guedalla, *Palmerston* (1926), p. 30; Minto, vol. 1, p. 167; K. Bourne, *Palmerston; the Early Years, 1784–1841* (1982), pp. 2–3.
[6] R. Connell, *Portrait of a Whig Peer: compiled from the papers of the Second Viscount Palmerston, 1739–1802* (1957), p. 267.
[7] J. Ridley, *Lord Palmerston* (1970), p. 14.
[8] Minto, vol. 3, p. 220.
[9] Minto, vol. 3, pp. 231, 235.
[10] W. Hamilton, *Collected Works of Dugald Stewart* (1877), vol. 8, pp. xxi–ii.
[11] Bourne, pp. 22–3.

Notes to Chapter 3

[1] H.L. Bulwer and E. Ashley, *Life of Viscount Palmerston* (1871–6), vol. 1, p. 370.
[2] *Hansard,* First Ser., X, 300–1 (3 Feb 1808); H.L. Bulwer and E. Ashley, ibid., vol. 1, p. 83.
[3] Bulwer and Ashley, vol. 1, pp. 85–7.
[4] B.P. GMC, Palmerston to Malmesbury, 16 Oct 1809; Malmesbury to Palmerston, 17 Oct 1809.
[5] P. Guedalla, *Palmerston* (1926), p. 60.
[6] Bulwer and Ashley, vol. 1, p. 128.
[7] K. Bourne, *Palmerston: the Early Years, 1784–1841* (1982), p. 115.
[8] Guedalla, p. 96.
[9] Quoted Bourne, pp. 133–4.
[10] Bulwer and Ashley, vol. 1, p. 150.
[11] *Hansard,* First Ser., XXIV, 971–6 (1 Mar 1813).
[12] Bulwer and Ashley, vol. 1, pp. 174–9.
[13] J. Ridley, *Lord Palmerston* (1970), p. 61.
[14] Bourne, pp. 256–64; K. Robbins, 'Palmerston, Bright and Gladstone in North Wales', *Transactions of the Caernarvonshire Historical Society,* 41 (1980) 129–30.
[15] Bourne, pp. 181–226.

Notes to Chapter 4

[1] H.L. Bulwer and E. Ashley, *Life of Viscount Palmerston* (1871–6), vol. 1, p. 377.
[2] *Hansard,* 1st Ser., XXXII 872–3 (26 Feb. 1816).
[3] BL. Add. MSS. Dudley to Aberdeen, 23 Apr. 1827.
[4] M.E. Chamberlain, *Lord Aberdeen: A Politcal Biography* (1983), pp. 205–7, 208, 213–14.
[5] *Hansard,* 2nd Ser., XXI 1664 (1 June 1829).
[6] He called them 'fierce, rascally, thieving, ignorant ragamuffins' who hated England, W. Hinde, *Canning* (1973), p. 376.
[7] Chamberlain, pp. 231–3.
[8] D. Southgate, *"The Most English Minister . . ." the policies and politics of Palmerston* (1966), p. 7.

[9] Quoted Hinde, p. 324.

[10] *Hansard,* 2nd Ser., XXI 1644–5, 1651.

[11] The most detailed analysis of Palmerston's attitude to parliamentary reform is still H.C.F. Bell, 'Palmerston and Parliamentary Representation', *Journal of Modern History,* IV (1932), 186–213.

[12] Bulwer, vol. 1, p. 383.

[13] Bell, *J.M.H.,* 188–90; BP, GC/Gr/1973.

Notes to Chapter 5

[1] C.K. Webster, *The Foreign Policy of Palmerston* (1951), vol. 1, p. 34.

[2] Quoted K. Bourne, *Palmerston: the Early Years 1784–1841* (1982), p. 314.

[3] Quoted J. Ridley, *Lord Palmerston* (1970), pp. 102–3.

[4] Bourne, p. 334. When a fire occurred in the Foreign Office in 1839, a clerk stuck his head into Palmerston's room, yelled 'take care of the Protocols' and withdrew before he could be identified.

[5] For details see Ridley, p. 134.

[6] Ridley, pp. 130–1, 135; H.L. Bulwer and E. Ashley, *Life of Viscount Palmerston* (1871–6), vol. 2, pp. 103–10.

[7] *Hansard,* 2nd Ser., XIV, 1045 (2 Aug 1832).

[8] Quoted Ridley, p. 140.

[9] Bulwer and Ashley, vol. 2, pp. 180, 186.

[10] The best discussion of this titanic struggle between Palmerston and Metternich is still C.K. Webster, 'Palmerston, Metternich and the European System', *Proceedings of the British Academy,* XX (1934), pp. 125–58.

[11] The full story is revealed for the first time in Bourne, p. 304.

[12] Quoted Webster, vol.1, pp. 283–4.

[13] *Hansard,* 3rd Ser., liii, 818, 925–50 (esp. 945) (8–9 Apr 1840).

[14] F.O. 84/376, Palmerston to Stevenson, 27 Aug 1841.

[15] C. Greville, (ed. H. Reeve) *Memoirs* (1888), vol. IV, pp. 308–9.

Notes to Chapter 6

[1] Quoted H.L.F. Bell, *Lord Palmerston* (1936), vol. 1, p. 330.

[2] C. Greville, (ed. H. Reeve) *Memoirs,* (1888), vol. 5, p. 111. For Palmerston's relations with the press at this time see S. Koss, *The Rise and Fall of the Political Press in Britain* (1981), vol. 1, pp. 45, 74–6.

[3] A.C. Benson (ed.), *Letters of Queen Victoria* (1908), vol. 2, pp. 67–8.

[4] Palmerston himself helped to originate the story. He expressed pleasure at 'the sweep made of the Plotters of the Spanish Marriages: and what is most poetical in the Retribution is that they have all of them been themselves the active agents of their own Destruction', quoted P. Guedalla, *Palmerston* (1926), p. 283. For a careful assessment of its truth see R. Bullen, *Palmerston, Guizot and the Collapse of the Entente Cordiale* (1974).

[5] H.L. Bulwer and E. Ashley, *Life of Viscount Palmerston* (1871–6), vol. 1, pp. 93–4.

[6] This was taken much more seriously by the Whig government than has generally been realized, see D.J.V. Jones, *The Last Rising: the Newport Insurrection of 1839,* (1985).

[7] B.P. GC/RU/1010, Palmerston to Russell, 26 Mar 1847.

[8] The whole sad story is told in detail, C. Woodham-Smith, *The Great Hunger* (1965), pp. 223–6.

[9] B.P. GC/RU/976, Palmerston to Russell, 3 Dec 1845.

[10] Ashley, vol. 1, p. 109.

[11] B.P. GC/RU/1047, Palmerston to Russell, 2 Aug 1848.

[12] *The Times,* 2 Aug 1847; *Speech of Lord Viscount Palmerston . . . to the Electors at Tiverton on the 31st July 1847,* Smith, Elder and Co., 1847; J. Ridley, *Lord Palmerston* (1970), pp. 323–7.

[13] Bulwer and Ashley, vol. 1, pp. 98, 110.

[14] B.P. GC/RU/1053, Palmerston to Russell, 9 Apr 1849.

[15] B.P. GC/RU/1956, Palmerston to Russell, 14 Sept 1849.

[16] Ridley, pp. 341–2; Bell, vol. 1, pp. 439–40.

[17] Bell, vol. 1, pp. 441–3.

[18] B.P. CG/WY/100, Palmerston to Wyse, 3 Dec 1849.

[19] B.P. GC/WY/101, Palmerston to Wyse, 12 Feb 1850.

[20] B.P. GC/WY/102, 104, Palmerston to Wyse, 4 Mar, 7 Mar, 19 Apr 1850.

[21] *Hansard,* 3rd Ser., cxii, 444, 586 (25, 27 June 1850).

[22] B.P. GC/RU/1053, Palmerston to Russell, 9 Apr 1849.

[23] Bulwer and Ashley, vol. 1, pp. 287–9.

[24] Palmerston's anger is illustrated by the fact that he kept a mass of press cuttings and letters of sympathy, carefully annotated in his own hand 'On my removal', B.P. GMC/47–106.

Notes to Chapter 7

[1] Graham Papers, 124, Graham to Aberdeen, 5 Aug 1852 and encls. For details of these complicated negotiations see M.E. Chamberlain, *Lord Aberdeen: A Political Biography* (1983), pp. 427–37.

[2] B.P. GC/LA/74, Lansdowne to Palmerston, 9 Oct 1852, Palmerston to Lansdowne, 'First week in October', 1852, 14 Oct 1852; /75 Lansdowne to Palmerston, 22 Oct 1852.

[3] B.P. GMC/47, Peter Borthwick to Palmerston, 27 Dec 1851.

[4] J. Vincent (ed), *Disraeli, Derby and the Conservative Party: the Political Journals of Lord Stanley, 1849–1869* (1978), pp. 37–8.

[5] H.L. Bulwer and E. Ashley, *Life of Viscount Palmerston* (1871–6), vol. 2, p. 5.

[6] Chamberlain, pp. 446–7. Contemporaries suspected that Lady Palmerston urged him to accept because they needed his official salary. Palmerston himself seems to have feared being left isolated, H.C.F. Bell, *Lord Palmerston* (1936), vol. 2, pp. 73–4.

[7] Graham Papers, 124, Diary, 23 Dec 1852; A.C. Benson (ed.), *Letters of Queen Victoria* (1908), vol. 2, p. 420.

[8] Duke of Argyll, *Autobiography and Memoirs* (1907), vol. 1, pp. 374–83; Ashley, vol. 2, pp. 6, 11.

[9] Bulwer and Ashley, vol. 3, pp. 127–9.
[10] B.P. HA/F/1/2/4/7/8; Bulwer and Ashley, vol. 2, p. 10.
[11] Bulwer and Ashley, vol. 2, pp. 13–14, 17.
[12] Palmerston to Gladstone, 20 Oct 1853, P. Guedalla (ed.) *Gladstone and Palmerston: being the Correspondence between Lord Palmerston and Mr Gladstone 1851–1865* (1928), pp. 95–6.
[13] For details see J. Ridley, *Lord Palmerston* (1970), pp. 411–12.
[14] Add. MSS. 43049, Palmerston to Aberdeen, 10 Feb 1853.
[15] Add. MSS. 43191, Palmerston to Graham, 29 May 1853, Aberdeen to Graham, 31 May 1853.
[16] Add. MSS. 43049, Palmerston to Aberdeen, 7 Oct 1853; Add. MSS. 43191, Aberdeen to Graham, 8 Oct 1853.
[17] B.P. GMC/130, Memorandum by Palmerston on conversation with Derby on 22 Feb 1852.
[18] Add. MSS. 43049, Palmerston to Aberdeen, 12 Feb 1854; cf. B.P. GC/RU/1108, Palmerston to Russell, 14 Nov 1853; B.P. HA/G/9, Palmerston to Russell, 29 Jan 1854.
[19] B.P. GC/RU/915, Palmerston to Russell, 22 Jan 1835.
[20] Add. MSS. 43048, Victoria to Aberdeen, 21 Dec 1853.
[21] Add. MSS. 43049, Palmerston to Aberdeen, 10 Dec 1853.

Notes to Chapter 8

[1] The best short account is D. Gillard, *The Struggle for Asia, 1828–1914: a study in British and Russian imperialism* (1977).
[2] Kingsley Martin, *The Triumph of Lord Palmerston: a study of public opinion in England before the Crimean War* (1963), p. 16.
[3] B.P. CAB/39, D'Urquhart to Melbourne, 6 Aug 1840.
[4] For a good account of Russophobia in general and Urquhart's role in particular, see A.J.P. Taylor, *The Troublemakers* (1957), pp. 42–50.
[5] S. Koss, *The Rise and Fall of the Political Press in Britain* (1981), vol. 1, p. 81.
[6] Kingsley Martin, pp. 85–6, 118–19.
[7] MSS Clar. Dep. C15, Palmerston to Clarendon, 4 Mar 1854; Add. MSS. 43068, Aberdeen to Russell, 27 Apr 1854.
[8] Add MSS. 43189, Clarendon to Aberdeen, 26 June 1854; RA G 17/89, Prince Albert, Memorandum, 7 Oct 1854.
[9] B.P. CAB/65–79. This crucial series of memoranda seems not to have been available to either J. Ridley, *Lord Palmerston* (1970), p. 429 or J.B. Conacher, *The Aberdeen Coalition 1852–1855: A Study in Mid Nineteenth Century Party Politics* (1968), pp. 452–3. Oddly enough Gladstone's memorandum was published in P. Guedalla, *Palmerston and Gladstone* (1928), pp. 97–8, where it gives the impression that he was pressing for the attack, instead of merely commentating on Palmerston's memorandum, which is not given.
[10] For discussion of the controversies surrounding that meeting see Conacher, pp. 452–3. The charge that several ministers fell asleep may well be true but the Cabinet was only ratifying decisions already arrived at.
[11] Add. MSS. 43191, Graham to Aberdeen, 28 June 1855.

[12] H.L. Bulwer and E. Ashley, *Life of Viscount Palmerston* (1871–6), vol. 2, pp. 76–7.

[13] *Hansard,* 3rd ser., vol. 144, 1840 (3 Mar 1857).

[14] H.C.F. Bell, *Lord Palmerston* (1936), vol. 2, pp. 173–4.

[15] *Hansard,* 3rd ser., vol. 144, 1391–1421, 1809–34 (26 Feb, 3 Mar 1857).

[16] E. Hodder, *Life and Works of the 7th Earl of Shaftesbury* (1887), vol. 3, p. 43 (9 Mar 1857).

Notes to Chapter 9

[1] C. Greville, (ed. H. Reeve) *Memoirs* (1888), vol. VIII, p. 259.

[2] A.R.D. Elliot, *Life of George Joachim Goschen, First Viscount Goschen, 1831–1907* (1911), vol. 1, p. 65.

[3] For a good discussion of the relationship of Palmerston and Gladstone see D. Steele, 'Gladstone and Palmerston, 1855–65' in *Gladstone, Politics and Religion* (ed. P.J. Jagger) (1985).

[4] For discussion of this see H.C.F. Bell, *Lord Palmerston* (1936), vol. 2, pp. 259–60 and J. Ridley, *Lord Palmerston* (1970), pp. 496–8.

[5] Quoted Ridley, p. 565.

[6] *Hansard,* 3rd ser., vol. 171, 1375 (23 June 1863).

[7] Ridley, pp. 499–501.

[8] Fitzmaurice, *Life of the Second Earl Granville* (1905), vol. 1, pp. 325–6.

[9] Bell, vol. 2, pp. 209–11.

[10] H.L. Bulwer and E. Ashley, *Life of Viscount Palmerston* (1871–8), vol. 2, pp. 168–72; Ridley, p. 495.

[11] Quoted D. Beales, *England and Italy, 1859–60* (1961), p. 68. This is the best analysis of Palmerston's policy towards Italy in this period.

[12] B.P. GC/RU/1127, Palmerston to Russell, 28 June 1859.

[13] Beales, pp. 117–24.

[14] For military aspects of the *Trent* affair see K. Bourne, *The Balance of Power in North America* (1967), pp. 210–47.

[15] Palmerston to Leopold, 15 Nov 1863, Bulwer and Ashley, vol. 2, pp. 236–42.

[16] *Hansard,* 3rd ser., vol. 172, 1252 (23 July 1863).

[17] Palmerston to Russell, 13 Feb 1864, Bulwer and Ashley, vol. 2, pp. 247–8.

[18] *Hansard,* 3rd ser., vol. 176, 709–50, 1198, 1272–87 (4, 8 July 1864): W.F. Monypenny and G.E. Buckle, *The Life of Benjamin Disraeli, Earl of Beaconsfield* (1910–20) vol. IV, pp. 345–7, 405.

[19] Palmerston to Russell, 13 September 1865, Bulwer and Ashley, vol. 2, pp. 270–1.

Notes to Chapter 10

[1] J. Vincent, *The Formation of the Liberal Party, 1857–68* (1966).

[2] B.P. GC/RU/1108, Palmerston to Russell, 14 Nov 1853; B.P. GC/LA/110, Palmerston to Lansdowne, 8 Dec 1853.

[3] D.F. Krein, *The Last Palmerston Government* (1978).

[4] *The Times,* 19, 21 Oct 1865.

[5] H.W.V. Temperley, *England and the Near East: The Crimea* (1964), pp. 59–60.
[6] B.L. Add. MSS. 43384, Bright to Cobden, 25 Oct 1860.
[7] *The Times,* 20 Oct 1865.

Bibliography

Manuscript Sources

Royal Archives, Windsor Castle.
Aberdeen Papers, British Library.
Bright Papers, British Library.
Broadlands Papers, Southampton University Library.
Clarendon Papers, Bodleian Library, Oxford.
Foreign Office Papers, Public Record Office.
Graham Papers, Bodleian Library, Oxford.
Russell Papers, Public Record Office.

Major biographies of Palmerston

E. Ashley – see H.L. Bulwer.
H.C.F. Bell, *Lord Palmerston,* 2 vols. Longmans, Green & Co., 1936.
K. Bourne, *Palmerston: the Early Years, 1784–1841,* Allen Lane, 1982.
H.L. Bulwer and E. Ashley, *Life of Viscount Palmerston,* 5 vols, Bentley, 1871–6.
P. Guedalla, *Palmerston,* Ernest Benn, 1926.
J. Ridley, *Lord Palmerston,* Constable, 1970.
D. Southgate, *"The Most English Minister . . .": the policies and politics of Palmerston,* Macmillan, 1966.

Selected published sources

M.S. Anderson, *The Eastern Question,* Macmillan, 1966.
Argyll, Duke of, *Autobiography and Memoirs,* 2 vols, Murray, 1907.
D. Beales, *England and Italy, 1859–60,* Nelson, 1961.
H.C.F. Bell, 'Palmerston and Parliamentary Representation', *Journal of Modern History,* IV (1932) 186–213.
A.C. Benson (ed.), *Letters of Queen Victoria, 1837–1861* (1st ser.), 3 vols, Murray, 1908.

K. Bourne, *The Balance of Power in North America*, Longman, 1967.
— — *The Foreign Policy of Victorian England, 1830–1902*, Clarendon, 1970.

G.E. Buckle (ed.), *Letters of Queen Victoria, 1862–1878*, (2nd ser.), 3 vols, Murray, 1926.

R. Bullen, *Palmerston, Guizot and the Collapse of the Entente Cordiale*, Athlone, 1974.

M.E. Chamberlain, *Lord Aberdeen: A Political Biography*, Longman, 1983.

J.B. Conacher, *The Aberdeen Coalition 1852–1855: A Study in Mid-Nineteenth Century Party Politics*, C.U.P., 1968.

B. Connell, *Portrait of a Whig Peer: compiled from the papers of the Second Viscount Palmerston, 1739–1802*, A. Deutsche, 1957.

B. Connell, *Regina v. Palmerston: the correspondence between Queen Victoria and her Foreign and Prime Minister, 1837–1865*, Evans Bros, 1962.

A.R.D. Elliott, *Life of George Joachim Goschen, First Viscount Goschen, 1831–1907*, 2 vols, Longmans, 1911.

E. Fitzmaurice, *Life of Granville George Leveson Gower, Second Earl Granville, 1815–1891*, 2 vols, Longman, 1905.

D. Gillard, *The struggle for Asia, 1828–1914: a study in British and Russian imperialism*, Methuen, 1977.

C. Greville, (ed. H. Reeve), *Memoirs*, 8 vols, Longmans, Green & Co., 1888.

P. Guedalla, *Gladstone and Palmerston: being the Correspondence between Lord Palmerston and Mr. Gladstone, 1851–1865*, Gollancz, 1928.

J. Hannay, 'The Family of Temple', *The Cornhill Magazine*, XII (1865) 749–60.

G.B. Henderson, *Crimean War Diplomacy and other Essays*, Glasgow University Publications LXVIII, 1947.

W. Hinde, *Canning*, Collins, 1973.

E. Hodder, *Life and Work of the 7th Earl of Shaftesbury*, 3 vols, Cassell, 1887.

A.G. Imlah, *Britain and Switzerland, 1845–60*, Longmans, 1966.

P. Kennedy, *The Rise of the Anglo-German Antagonism, 1860–1914*, Allen and Unwin, 1980.

S. Koss, *The Rise and Fall of the Political Press in Britain*, vol 1, *The Nineteenth Century*, Hamish Hamilton, 1981.

D.F. Krein, *The Last Palmerston Government*, Iowa State University Press, 1978.

B. Kingsley Martin, *The Triumph of Lord Palmerston: a study of public opinion in England before the Crimean War*, Hutchinson, rev. ed., 1963.

C.R. Middleton, *The Administration of British Foreign Policy, 1782–1846,* Duke U.P., 1977.

Minto, Earl of, *Life and Letters of Sir Gilbert Elliot, First Earl of Minto,* (ed. Countess of Minto), 3 vols, Longmans, Green & Co., 1874.

W.F. Monypenny and G.E. Buckle, *The Life of Benjamin Disraeli, Earl of Beaconsfield,* 6 vols, 1910–20.

J. Morley, *Life of Gladstone,* 2 vols, Macmillan, 1903.

N. Rich, *Why the Crimean War?* University Press of New England, 1985.

K. Robbins, 'Palmerston, Bright and Gladstone in North Wales', *Transactions of the Caernarvonshire Historical Society,* 4 (1980) 129.

B. Semmel, *Liberalism and Naval Strategy: Ideology, Interest and Sea Power during the Pax Britannica,* Allen and Unwin, 1986.

C. Sproxton, *Palmerston and the Hungarian Revolution,* C.U.P., 1919.

D. Steele, 'Gladstone and Palmerston, 1855–65', in *Gladstone, Politics and Religion* (ed. P.J. Jagger), Macmillan, 1985, pp. 117–47.

— — 'Palmerston's Foreign Policy and Foreign Secretaries 1855–1865', in *British Foreign Secretaries and Foreign Policy: From Crimean War to First World War* (ed. K.M. Wilson), Croom Helm, 1987.

A.J.P. Taylor, *The Italian Problem in European Diplomacy, 1847–1849,* Manchester University Press, 1934.

A.J.P. Taylor, *The Troublemakers,* Hamish Hamilton, 1957.

H.W.V. Temperley, *England and the Near East: the Crimea,* Cass reprint, 1964.

J. Vincent, *Disraeli, Derby and the Conservative Party: the Political Journals of Lord Stanley, 1849–1869,* Harvester Press, 1978.

J. Vincent, *The Formation of the Liberal Party, 1857–1868,* Constable, 1966.

C.K. Webster, *The Foreign Policy of Palmerston, 1830–1841,* 2 vols, G. Bell & Sons, 1951.

— — 'Palmerston, Metternich and the European System', *Proceedings of the British Academy,* XX (1934) 125–58.

C. Woodham-Smith, *The Great Hunger,* New English Library, 1965.

The Author

Reader in History at the University College of Swansea, Dr Muriel
Chamberlain is a native of Leicestershire, a Fellow of the Royal Historical
Society and a Member of the Council of the Historical Association. Her
other publications include *The Scramble for Africa* (1974), *British Foreign
Policy in the Age of Palmerston* (1980), *Lord Aberdeen: A Political
Biography* (1983), and *Decolonization: the Fall of the European Empires*
(1985).

The General Editor

Kenneth O. Morgan F.B.A., D.Litt., is Fellow and Praelector of The
Queen's College, Oxford. Born in Middlesex of north Cardiganshire and
Meirionethshire origins he is an eminent historian and prolific author. He
has written extensively and authoritatively on Radical movements in
nineteenth-century and early twentieth-century Britain; his titles include
Wales in British Politics 1868–1922 (1963), *David Lloyd George* (1963),
Keir Hardie (1975), *Rebirth of a Nation: Wales 1880–1980* (1981) and
Labour in Power 1945–1951 (1984). He has been editor of *The Welsh
History Review* since 1965 and was elected a Fellow of the British Academy
in 1983.